CHAOS & ASH

KENDALL JOHNSON

PELEKINESIS

NEW YORK † LONDON † SYDNEY † LOS ANGELES

Chaos & Ash by Kendall Johnson

ISBN: 978-1-949790-38-2
eISBN: 978-1-949790-39-9

Layout and book design by Mark Givens
Artwork by Kendall Johnson

"First Firefight," "The Ridge," "Evensong," "Marines: January 2002, Manhattan," "Grand Rounds," "Revival Sunday," "O'Brien's Boat," and "Healing Dr. Morella Joseph" contain excerpts from the field journals of Kendall Johnson

"First Firefight" appeared in *Worthing Flash Fiction* in the UK, Jan. 2020

Portions of "Revival Sunday" and "O'Brien's Boat" appeared previously in Johnson, Kendall, *Fragments: An Archeology of Memory,* Inland Empire Museum of Art. (2017)

First Pelekinesis Printing 2020

For information:
Pelekinesis, 112 Harvard Ave #65, Claremont, CA 91711 USA

Library of Congress Cataloging-in-Publication Data

Names: Johnson, Kendall, 1945- author.
Title: Chaos & ash / Kendall Johnson.
Other titles: Chaos and ash
Description: New York : Pelekinesis, [2020]
Identifiers: LCCN 2020008331 (print) | LCCN 2020008332 (ebook) | ISBN 9781949790382 (paperback) | ISBN 9781949790399 (epub)
Subjects: LCSH: Johnson, Kendall, 1945- | Disasters--Psychological aspects--Case studies. | Psychic trauma--Case studies. | Post-traumatic stress disorder--Case studies.
Classification: LCC BF789.D5 J644 2020 (print) | LCC BF789.D5 (ebook) | DDC 155.9/35--dc23
LC record available at https://lccn.loc.gov/2020008331
LC ebook record available at https://lccn.loc.gov/2020008332

www.pelekinesis.com

CHAOS & ASH

Kendall Johnson

Contents

PART III: LIGHT ANGELS AND DARK

PART IV: STANDING DOWN

SECTION VII: LETTERS UPON RETIREMENT

EPILOGUE

With grateful thanks, this book is dedicated to two people:
the first is my wife Susie Ilsley who endures my reading,
applauds my attempts, and prompts me to go farther.
Also to John Brantingham who leads me toward my own
uncharted paths.

Introduction

A freshly licensed psychotherapist, I was two years into my new clinical specialty as trauma therapist. In my private practice I treated varied psychic aches and bruises, sometimes referred by employers, sometimes by patients themselves. As a former firefighter and veteran, though, I found something missing in my teaching and clinical practice. It had taken years of education and training to get there, but an itch was going unscratched. On a whim I'd talked my way into a training session run by a former paramedic turned psychologist, who had established a national organization of psychological support professionals and paraprofessionals serving fire departments. "Critical incident stress" was a new term coined to describe events likely to result in lasting psychological distress or injury. Intervening in those events so as to mitigate critical incident stress and rebuild the human networks ruptured by those events became my new mission.

I grew with that organization as it grew to serve police, military, and other outfits both nationally and internationally. I eventually became a trainer for them, applying their principles to school settings, and sat on the editorial board of their journal. That organization is now known as the International Critical Incident Stress Foundation[i].

Up until 1986 the incidents I dealt with, while dramatic, were essentially small. I'd been called into two light aircraft crashes with no fatalities, several deaths of civilians where governmental employees had been involved, two employee suicides

---

i   International Critical Incident Stress Foundation https://icisf.org/

and the case of one employee released from prison to return to work. Intense, of course, but only involving a handful of individuals involved in incidents which were largely over by the time I got there. My training had involved a follow-up debriefing of emergency crews who had responded to the crash of passenger flight Air Florida 90 which had pancaked into the frozen Potomac River following take-off from National Airport in DC. I knew things could get bigger.

In 1987 the scope of the incidents I took part in began to change. Several factors came into play. Incidents began to grow in size. That was the year of the lightning storm that swept California and started hundreds of fires, particularly in the northern part of the state. There was also a qualitative change, however. Due to widening and increasingly volatile news reporting, civilian opinion reached out of the cities and into the wildland. Big-incident management became more aggressive with managing information and news as well as community relations. The size of incidents continued to grow—the next years saw mega-fires in Yellowstone and Idaho. These fires were enormous, but also in terms of the political pressure that accompanied them.

The age of public spectacle sought out Smokey Bear.

The traumas themselves also shifted in nature. As disasters became TV fodder, it became *de rigueur* and politically expedient to include psychological consultants as part of the response team. With the increased attention to child and domestic abuse, more clinicians were becoming involved in extra-clinic practice. Their backgrounds often included store-front, police, and hospital outreach, but rarely included boots-on-the-ground fire or disaster experience. As a result, I began to be called to work in disaster settings—earthquakes, storms, flooding—and schools as well, due to my teaching experience. I was called to develop a curriculum for the training of crisis responders in schools across the country. Human suffering had become a major industry.

At that point things turned darker. I was called upon by police departments to deal with the psychological fallout from officer ambushes and near deaths. I worked with ambulance crews and crisis team members who were responding to human-caused disasters such as domestic and foreign terrorism. I even took part in multi-agency management of particularly volatile events such as serial killers or cannibalization. Hollywood was making money scaring people, but many of their plots were not made up.

The world itself became a darker place for me during my twenty-five year tour as an on-scene critical incident consultant. Every career can be assessed by the calculus of gains and losses, what one is able to get accomplished and the price one and one's family have to pay. The work played into my past and shaped the way I viewed the world. The following stories explore that work, which to me became a personal crucible.

Kendall Johnson, Ph.D.
431 W. Arrow Highway
Claremont, California 91711
kjohns@gmail.com
909 438-2156

October 16, 1986

Christopher Williams, Th.D.
1936 E Rte 66
San Dimas, CA 91740

Re: Letter of Introduction

Dear Dr. Williams:

This is to introduce myself and to request clinical supervision. I'm a therapist, with a clinical specialty in trauma. I teach as well. Recently I was trained in workplace crisis intervention and am thinking of developing a consulting practice as an adjunct to my clinical work. Given the sometimes intense and personal nature of this work I think it wise to obtain supervision. You come highly recommended, and I believe your background in the military, as a truck driver, and as an Episcopal Priest will prove helpful; my work contexts would likely be challenging to a supervisor who works strictly with white collar and professional clients in protected settings. I hope to be able to work in the contexts of emergency service, military, and disaster.

Let me give you a brief outline of my background. I hold a doctorate in clinical psychology, teach, and have a small private therapy practice. More importantly, perhaps, during my undergraduate work I dropped out of college and fought fires for three seasons with the US Forest Service and then served with the Navy in Vietnam, before returning to school. I feel these experiences will be important in determining my ability to pursue incident consultation. I'm hoping you will be able to help me keep my own background in perspective, as I found the fire fighting, in particular, engaging and formative to me as a young man.

I look forward to hearing from you and setting up an initial appointment.

Sincerely yours,

Kendall Johnson

Christopher Williams, Th.D.
1936 E Rte 66
San Dimas, CA 91740

October 19, 1986

Kendall Johnson, Ph.D.
431 W. Arrow Highway
Claremont, California 91711

Re: Letter of Invitation

Dear Dr. Johnson,

Glad you wrote requesting Clinical Supervision. I like supervising clinicians and you sound like you are getting into some interesting work. I've been longing for something more fun than my normal neurotics and whiners. You might not know this, but I am certified to provide supervision at two of the local graduate schools.

Let's meet at my office in San Dimas in a couple of weeks and we'll talk details.

Yours,

Christopher Williams, Th.D.

P.S. I read somewhere that Norman Maclean is working on a new book investigating the Mann Gulch Fire in 1949. I read that it'll probably take him a couple of years to finish it because the information is locked away and he's working slowly. You might enjoy it when it comes out.

PART I

In The Field

The phrase "in the field" is a term used by professionals—be they military, emergency responders, teachers, people in the ministry, psychologists, or any of several other career groups. Used by these folks it doesn't mean working within the discipline, it means working where the boots of that discipline actually walk trails: the real world. The street. Military folk are not said to be in the field when they serve in the Pentagon, or even on a military base in Texas or Alaska, nor are psychologists when they are in their office, laboratory, clinic, or classroom. On the other hand, if the psychologist drives or flies to a command center or even a gathering of workers drinking coffee in a break room, or rides along with a single individual in the performance of his or her duty—following exposure to an incident that was overwhelming—that psychologist can be said to be in the field. As part of my practice I served in the field.

A friend once asked me why I liked to get my hands dirty, eating in fire camps or base chow halls or gas station vending machines, why I enjoyed working with firefighters, law enforcement, and rescuers in distress. I told him it had to do with smelling burning pine incense, hearing trumpets, and getting into the wild. Hell, I didn't know. It started on a firefight a half century ago, watching an entire mountain burn so hot at night that the tall trees exploded from overheated resin, and the resulting sounds of cannon fire echoed in the darkness. Shiva's dance drew me like a magnet—still does, if I'm honest—because out there is the magic.

Supervisory Verbatim #1:

My Plan

"So let me see if I got this all straight," said Dr. Christopher Williams, Th.D. "You want me to provide clinical supervision to you as you build your practice, right?"

"Yes." I answered.

"And that practice specializes in treating psychological trauma as well as on-scene intervention following critical incidents, events that overwhelm people and may leave lasting traumatic symptoms?"

"As well as difficulties that keep their work team from operating as effectively as they did before the incident," I added.

He thought for a minute. "This is interesting. But why? This will likely be stressful for you, and I understand that's why you'll see me. Most people want to leave situations such as you describe as fast as they can. So let me ask you again: What brings you here? What is it that draws you to this kind of work?"

First Firefight

I felt imprisoned by school and had to break out, a tender moth hell-bent to leap into the flame. The US Forest Service was rich with promise. I would shed my books, sweaters, and myopia, and take up arms in a gloriously moral equivalent of war: fighting forest fires. I signed on, purchased uniforms, did my push-ups and hill climbs, suffered abuse from my mentors, learned what I could in fire school, set up housekeeping in the East Fork barracks, worked on projects, and . . . waited. It seemed as if I would never see what I'd come for. Finally, in late October we were dispatched to a big one.

1964, Santa Barbara, California. We are setting up to protect houses in an oak-covered canyon at night, and our hose defenses are in place. It had been insane so far. We'd almost gotten cooked twice, and the fire had burned right through our fire camp. Now we are getting ready to save these homes built in an indefensible tunnel of trees their owners thought would never burn.

Standard Run and Gun, we'd been directed; the fire is approaching from uphill, so protect the house on the top till the fire goes past, then pull back to the next. Things have worked differently. The fire has blown underneath us by the crazy wind, and it is at least 95 degrees in the middle of the night. A deep glow surrounds us, diffused by the thickening smoke. The rest of the crew is positioned around the structure. I am standing on the road above the house, my hose hooked up to a hydrant—an unlimited water source. My job is to put out the spots and keep it from crossing. I am impatient.   It comes like a screaming red tornado. The flames are thirty or forty feet high as the preheated brush and scrub oak nearly explodes. In a minute the entire uphill side is burning, and sparks and burning debris cascade down to the other side. I alternate hitting the spots below me with a straight stream and trying to cool down the wall of flame. It gets hotter.

And better. Any idiot would be terrified, but I find myself turned on. Oblivious to the obvious danger, not caring that I am driven to my knees with the intense reflective heat from the flames on both sides, I take joy in holding my ground. No longer caring at all that the fire had jumped the road and was on the verge of creating a total rout, I am lost in the fight. The outcome simply doesn't matter. The doors to hell have been breached, and I lose myself in the passionate embrace of the unholy. I truly love it here.

Perhaps Nirvana is the product of Shiva's sword and not quiet contemplation. Surrounded by twisting entrails of flame, where the light has become silver and an angelic chorus sings beyond hearing, I have finally found the navel of the world. This is the center of the holy city, the eye of God. I have come home to a place I'd never imagined, to a time without time. Eternity, it seems, has come to life.

I become aware of a frantic beating on my back and helmet, and hands begin to drag me backwards. "Oh, no," I think, "Not now, I finally just got here!"

"Hey," Coop hollers in my ear, "It's time to boogie!"

I reluctantly fall back from the point position, dragging the hose as I go.

"Drop it, Stupid!" yells John. I didn't know he is here too. They each grab my coat by the shoulders and shove me rudely back down the road toward the engine. The fire is burning everywhere, and I see the Captain disconnecting hoses from the engine. Evidently he had sent Coop and John to retrieve me. We are going to retreat.

"You're damn lucky we found you," shouts John as we run. "We almost left you here!"

Above Santa Barbara

Coyote Fire, 1964

The third night came, and we were stuck on patrol. The fire was pretty much out in our sector; snags would occasionally pop and flare up, and we could see the glow coming over the ridge from the head of the fire as it made runs up small canyons. At 3:00 a.m. our area was quiet, and as the fog moved in, it was starting to get cold. We could hear animals moving about in the darkness and had heard of crews in this area getting charged by wild pigs. We bundled in blankets against the cold and stretched out on the hose racks on the engine.

Everyone else had fallen into a restless sleep, but the images of all the helicopters unloading firefighters on stretchers into ambulances in fire camp yesterday wouldn't leave me. We had heard about the burn-over, but I didn't expect so many of us to be hurt. None of the two hand-crews that were burned had died yet, but I couldn't shake the memory of what I'd learned in fire school— that most fire deaths are caused by the inhalation of hot gasses that seared the lungs and formed water blisters. You died only days later when you coughed and they broke. Out there at the end of the world, alone on a cold night, I thought of drowning on a hospital bed and prayed for a glorious, and very quick, ending.

I gradually became aware of an approaching truck's laboring transmission whine as it rounded the corner a half-mile down the canyon, and it was some time before its headlights lit the fog into an otherworldly glow . . . "It wasn't a truck at all, but a battered brown and white De Soto station wagon. The rest of the crew didn't start stirring until it pulled up beside the engine, making more dust than fog. The headlight glare looked like the second coming."

Howdy!" the civilian called out. We figured he was lost, and considering he'd just disrupted the first sleep we'd had in two and a half days, he was lucky we didn't roll him back down the mountain. "It's cold up here; thought you'd like some hot coffee and sandwiches." He had our attention.

"Got any cigarettes?" The captain always seemed on top of things.

"Sure!" If he had cigarettes, his cheer could be forgiven. He jumped out, slammed the car door, and lowered the back gate of the station wagon. This guy was set up for business. We climbed down off the engine. Coffee was in thermoses, sandwiches were fresh, and he was packing Marlboro reds and Lucky Strikes. Obviously a good man. "You guys did a lot for us down below last night," he explained, "the folks figured you might not have gotten any dinner."

We didn't say much but dug into the sandwiches. The coffee was hot. We stood around, finishing off the candy bars and pocketing the smokes.

"So how's the fire going?" the stranger asked, obviously to get a conversation going.

"Well, it's going pretty good it seems," the Captain quipped, unwilling to disclose anything important to a civilian, "it's pushing us around pretty good."

"I don't know," the civilian smiled, "I watched you down below last night. You guy's looked pretty good!"

"Yup." The Captain grinned at Coop, who looked away, "Tell that to the overhead."

I remembered Coop last night waking up behind the wheel after driving three blocks. We all shifted around some, still stinging from the rebuke we had received from the Sector Boss after falling asleep on the engine.

"Hey," the civilian started again, "Overhead's always like

that." We waited to see where he was going to go with that. He was a civilian, but again, he had brought coffee. He told a really funny story about his time in Korea that reminded us of our Sector Boss. We all chuckled, and John snorted coffee through his nose. "You guys want any more coffee?"

This guy was OK.

He closed up shop and climbed back into his De Soto. "Hey," he called out the window, "how far is the next engine?"

"Bear right at the fork, and then another few hundred yards. Can't miss it." The Engineer said. "Who you with?"

"Salvation Army," he smiled, then put the De Soto in gear, and drove off, down the road and into the fog.

"Copy that," the Captain nodded.

The Ridge

Years afterward, I studied Fredrich Nietzche, the 19th Century German existential philosopher who once described human evolution as a solitary climb up a bitter ridge, where Zarathustra inevitably encountered a terrible serpent whom he must defeat to go on. The snake was wholly other, the dark side of humankind that caused the strongest to quail. With no tools or weapons, Zarathustra's only way to defeat the snake was to do the unthinkable: to bite it's head off. To do so meant to take it into his mouth. To expose himself to the taste, feel, and smell of it.

Day 7

Lying on the fire camps disposable paper sleeping bags in the direct sun made my two hours of sleep less than worthless. Two hours of sleep after two straight days. The ground was hard, and the camp was noisy with the day's work going on around hundreds of sleeping forms. A single star hotel was luxurious in comparison. Still, it was hard to return to consciousness. I didn't know if I could go back out on the line, or what would happen if I did.

The jumble of mixed sounds coalesced into the droning "thump-thump" of helicopters coming and going, and the wails of sirens. Not more engine sirens, though, these were different. Ambulances, that was it. Helicopters and ambulances. Shit. I walked down to the edge of the bluff to look over the landing field, and there they were, the Dalton Hot Shots—one of the toughest crews in the country—bunched together like sheep in the shade thrown by the few eucalyptus trees separating the fire camp from the lower field. They were quiet and staring, which was unsettling to me, because it was not their normal, rowdy ebullience. In fact, while some were standing and some sitting or kneeling, they were close enough together to actually be touching shoulders. I walked up to see what was going on, and a couple of them looked up and nodded to me.

One of the squad bosses gestured toward the bottom field; "Check it out, man." The helicopters were landing in turns, each carrying two stretchers fixed to the sides of the skids. Each stretcher contained a strapped-in body wrapped in army blankets. As the choppers landed, medical crewmen ran under the blades, detached the stretchers, and carried them back to the ambulances where the stretchers were shoved in the back. The ambulances pulled out, obviously heading for the hospitals, and new stretchers were attached to the helicopters. The copters took off again, heading back toward the fire.

We pulled the night shift, and the captain was getting our assignment from Operations. Nobody was happy about it because of this morning's burn-over. We all fear the moment we are overtaken by fire and it felt like there was a jinx on this fire. Talk around camp was that there was something spooky about it. Vicious. It was as if there was some score to be settled, and the fire wasn't finished with us yet. The closer it came to sunset, the quieter we got.

Day 8
Sunday, Afternoon

Another double duty; night shift was extended into the next day. By mid-afternoon on the eighth day the fire had not only over-run our stand at the saddle, jumped our line, and dropped burning embers in the tall brush and scrub oak all down the slope behind us; those resulting spots had coalesced into a formidable run back up at us from our lee. We had previously moved our engines into a safe zone a quarter mile down the truck trail to engage the fire with hand tools. This came back to haunt us. We were cut off from our engines by the new erratic and unpredictable behavior of the fire. It seemed to be out-thinking us. There was only one way we could flee the encroaching circle of flame—up the hill.

We ran back up our laboriously-constructed but now worthless fire-line, then back along the truck trail. And when that got too hot, up the ridge itself. We climbed and coughed, no longer able to see where we were going. Each firefighter scrambled up the rocky slope—his tool prodding the next to move faster away from the heat. As the smoke became thicker, we simply moved uphill, despite the fact that we could no longer see where we had been or where we were going. Our eyes burned and teared up, snot ran down our faces and mixed with sweat, dust, and soot. Our goggles filled up and fogged over. Our bodies screamed for more oxygen. It wasn't clear whether the real enemy was now the fire or the panic.

And then we ran out of hillside. Multiple columns of smoke were joining, obscuring both sun and sky, and there was nowhere else to go. We stood together heaving and confused. The captains and more experienced crew bosses called for us to trench in, and we dug furiously into the rocks and soil to create a horizontal furrow just below the ridge in which to lay when the fire came. The ground did not cooperate. By the time the fire caught us, our trench was less than a foot deep with the dirt piled on the downhill edge to shield us from the heat. At the crew bosses' urging, we threw ourselves down, lying with our heads in the next person's feet, our tools covering our shoulders as we shoved our bandana-covered faces into the dirt.

Then the fire came, sweeping over us by inches, sucking the oxygen right out of our lungs. Our clothing spontaneously erupted, and we slapped out the fire on the legs of the next person while feeling our own legs being pummeled from behind.

The sound of a forest fire rivals that of a jet aircraft. It is a deep moan, a train too close, the collective groaning cry of thousands of plants in an unwilling, transfigurative dance. When the fire is upon you, you can barely make out your friend's screams, or discern them from your own.

The fire wasn't the final enemy. A more pervasive threat began to weave itself around and through the crew, an insidious black threat from ourselves that came up from within. It was fear. Not the frightful scares of sudden surprise, nor the over-concern of one who realizes inevitable pain or loss. This began as sickening dread of ending and pain and escalated wildly toward self-compromising panic. The air was gone, replaced by a burning gas that scorched the throat and refused to reach the lungs. Fighting to breathe, we watched the speckled lights flicker and the darkness began. Despite our determination to stay put, despite our terrible need to show that we could manage, chaos writhed within and we each began a countdown until we had to bolt. The black serpent of chaos and cowardice writhed within and our claims of dignity evaporated in the face of it.

Our leaders knew this. "Stay in the trench!" came the word down the line. "Stay there! Don't run!" I tried to focus instead on the ground inches in front of my face. Small rootlets lay bare, grasses that would now never be. A tiny ant ran in circles, trying to find safety, not comprehending the enormity of his predicament. I covered it with a handful of dirt. How odd, I thought, that it would likely live longer than me.

The boots ahead of me were jerking spasmodically, and I realized his pants had again started to burn. I beat his legs with my gloved hands, wondering if it really mattered, wondering if his legs hurt as much as mine, wondering if I could stay here longer.

The urge to run swept over me like an obsession, and I realized I was kicking now, although it wasn't clear whether it was in response to the burn or the urge to run. I felt as if I were covered with blankets and being strangled. The feet ahead were moving again, and I held them down. Something was battering my helmet, and someone else was yelling.

"Move, goddamn it, move out now!" I looked up to find a crew boss I did not recognize crouching over me. The air thudded with another sound: helicopter blades. "Go! Go!" he screamed. Where did his knowledge come from, his certainty? I ran.

The crew moved upward quickly, crouching low as they ran over the top of the ridge in groups. Somehow, the helicopters had broken through to pick us up. The wind had shifted, allowing windows of sky to appear through the acrid, ochre smoke. I was led through the haze to an army green Huey helicopter that had somehow nudged up parallel to the ridge and precariously balanced its left skid against a rock outcropping. Its blades were too close to the mountain.

"Drop your tool and go!" the boss shouted. *Never leave your tool,* I remembered being hammered into us in fire school.

Despite the cacophony of the fire and the helicopters, sounds seemed muffled and time slowed down. Great brown columns of smoke rose in helical plumes entwining one another. The captain appeared before us with a detached look, staring. A thin smile broke through his blackened face as if he were laughing at a private joke, and tears had coursed down the sides, washing white streaks on either side of his cheeks. He waved us forward, an actor in a slowing silent movie.

As we loped by him, he took each of us by the arm and pointed us toward the bird. It was strangely quiet as I came up to him. His eyes moved behind me, probably to gauge how close the fire was, yet they seemed to fix on something further off, beyond the pursuing wall of flame. His gaze slowly traveled back to fix on mine.

We stared at one another as I glided by, a knowledge passing between us. It wasn't clear to me what was transpiring in that moment, but it was something about centuries and lifetimes and lives gone beyond. I had never thought of him as a particularly deep man before, but in that brief moment of recognition, I realized he had been on this very spot before, and that he had danced with this same snake. I had just been received into this etheric dimension.

Heat again grew intense. I scrambled behind the others, ducking below and around the barely-visible copter's blade. I dove into the open door and was pulled in by strong hands.

We jammed into the seatless chopper, pulling yet another person in, and grabbing for support. The pilot immediately broke away from the mountain, and we were airborne. Making way for the next ship. The pilot swung us into the huge convection column. Immediately the visibility closed again. The helicopter attempted to push through toward light. We were slammed sharply upward, and almost immediately slammed more brutally back down again. Rocks and brush appeared dead ahead through the haze, the horizon disappearing crazily into the sky hard to the right. We dove and were sharply swept up again. It wasn't clear who was screaming and who was throwing up, but we clung together trying not to pitch out the door.

Suddenly everything went blue. We burst out of the smoke and into sunlight. As we continued the circle to the right, we saw two more helicopters darting through windows of smoke to pull the remainder of our crew off the ridge.

The fire had taken the entire mountain.

Clinical Verbatim #2:

Moth to Flame

"And you think that's normal?" asked Dr. Williams, fixing me with the sort of clinical gaze intended to cut through self-delusion and get to the nub of things; the secular psychologist's whack on the side of the head. I was seeing him as a clinical supervisor because I was being called to larger and larger incidents as a trauma consultant. "You're being drawn to these large incidents?" I'd just finished telling him about my first firefight when I was in the US Forest Service. Maybe I had embellished it a little, or worse, maybe not. He took a sip of his coffee. "So why do you think you needed to do all that?"

That is the question, I guess. Was my own clinical interest in trauma based on my own personal needs? Was I still seeking to recreate that first firefight? Clinical supervision is standard practice for therapists, particularly those who work in difficult areas. Even though my crisis management consultation was only part-time in addition to my teaching, it was trying enough to warrant supervision. I was there to keep my perspective, and that included keeping track of my own reactions. If I did have some driving inner need to do this work, then was I setting myself up for, in Dr. Williams' words, "major damage"?

"So, what else did you learn on that fire in Santa Barbara," he asked, "or are you still that moth in search of a nice, hot flame?"

"There's more," I muttered. "I learned some more on the ridge." I told him about it. "I learned that I loved being there, being in that kind of situation." It had been in some way a hallowed ground. I just couldn't put it to words.

"So that's what got you into this trauma work? That fire?" I sensed that Dr. Christopher Williams, Th.D., seemed delighted with so many targets of clinical opportunity. "How long ago was that fire?"

"Maybe twenty years." Maybe I was crazier than I thought.

"Why?" he asked. I thought Dr. Williams figured that I wanted him to find an itch that needed scratching, a nail needing pounding. Or maybe I just underestimated this truck driver turned Episcopal priest turned therapist. "Just don't sit there, tell me a story like that, and then expect me not to ask a few questions. Like why you would race off in the middle of the night to follow sirens."

"Well, it pays pretty well, and I think I'm doing something worthwhile."

"Adrenaline is a powerful, addictive agent, and adrenaline junkies abound. Look at the crazies who jump out of perfectly good airplanes for fun. The question I have for you, however, is this: Do you get yourself into these situations with your work for the pay or for the excitement?"

"It's both, I guess."

"And does it have a negative impact on your day job?"

"My teaching?" I asked. "Once in a while." I was thinking of the time I had to walk out of a staff meeting at the beginning of school because I had just come from meeting privately in my practice with a firefighter who had been in one of the big fires in Idaho where three crews had been burned over and their incident commanders had needed to fight for hose and for use of the sole helicopter available for all three fires. The teachers in my meeting had been arguing over which classroom needed the extra pencils.

"How about your family? Happy with how things are at home?"

I was quiet. "I hope I didn't give you the impression that I consider myself a paragon of mental health," I replied, shifting in my seat. "I don't."

"But that begs the question here, doesn't it?" He leaned forward. "This isn't about deciding if you're OK, it's about deciding what *you need*."

I stared at Dr. Williams, wondering what he was getting at. "What do you mean?" I asked.

John and the Captain

Sometimes we are distinguished more through the foibles of others than through our own glory. I may have come into my own as a firefighter on the Coyote Fire in 1964, but it was John who made me look good. I longed for promotion to the expected engineer/driver position coming up, and I was afraid that John would edge me out.

John came onto the East Fork engine crew as a replacement for Bob Whitney, who left to return to college. John had already put in a couple seasons as a firefighter, and that made me look bad because I needed badly to prove myself. I was the gung-ho junior crewman the captain favored. I gave the basic classes on fire behavior and pump hydraulics during our Sunday morning training sessions at the station. I taught the crew how to use rock climbing techniques to pull stranded hikers off the crumbly cliffs of East Fork. While I was working double time, though, John was brown-nosing anyone who'd listen, trading war stories to avoid hard work. He'd disappear when work had to be done and wouldn't keep the barracks clean. I wondered if the captain could see that John was really a slacker.

Then came our call to the Coyote Fire in Santa Barbara. Into the evening on the third day, we had been part of the multi-engine sector team that had stopped the fire from ripping through Montecito, just to the south of Santa Barbara. With the fire beaten back, we were assigned patrol, which we welcomed because, with luck, we might catch a nap. We hadn't slept in over fifty hours. As soon as we'd driven our sector, we found a place to park. The captain and the engineer/driver Cooper settled down in the cab, John curled up on the crew seat between the covered cab and the hose rack, and I climbed up on the hose rack. Even with the radio chatter from the outside speaker in my ear, I fell into a deep sleep.

Suddenly there was a big light in my eyes and someone was yelling. Struggling to make sense, I finally decided it was a flashlight, and that the sector chief was shouting something about rolling out the crew and heading up the road a quarter mile. The fire had broken out again and was making a run up the hill. I tried going back to sleep, but he kept it up. I slid down onto the crew seat, kicked John into an upright position, and then swung down to wake the captain. He finally woke up, shook Cooper and the engineer, and told him to back the engine up so that we could and get to the fire.

The captain walked to the rear of the engine where he could signal to Cooper that it was safe to back up. I climbed back up to the hose rack to get my gloves, and remembered the look of growing confusion on the captain's face as Cooper ignored his signals and drove off straight ahead. I saw the captain waving frantically as the engine gained speed, heading down the road toward town. I clung to the hose rack, waiting for Cooper to stop. Maybe he was looking for a place to turn around and go back.

Maybe not. We drove through the first lighted intersection at forty miles an hour. Cooper hit the red lights but not the siren. I started climbing down into the crew seat. John slept on. Because the exterior speaker was still on, I could hear the captain yelling on the sector chief's radio for Cooper to stop. We had a problem.

I climbed over John, stopping to belt him in. Then I climbed outside of the engine into the cold wind and, standing on the running board, worked my way along the side of the cab to the driver's door. When we blew through the next intersection, the cop directing traffic gestured wildly for opposing traffic to stop and then dove out of the way. We must have been doing sixty. Pulling myself up to Cooper's window, I looked in. His eyes were open, but he was expressionless. I screamed at him. Nothing. Cooper was driving in his sleep.

Reaching in through the window, I hit him. He looked sharply in my direction, then snapped forward again. This time his eyes got big and he hit the brakes. I somehow held on as the big truck slide slightly sideways to a stop. Cooper, at least when awake, could really drive.

When we got back to where we had left the captain, he was not pleased. I didn't say much, and Cooper didn't either. John managed to come up with a perfectly plausible story about how we couldn't find a decent place to turn around for four miles. The captain just looked at me, and I could tell he wanted to ask more, but I looked away. He wouldn't have believed it anyway.

Just as the sector chief had said, the spot fire was just down the road. Heavy brush, thick. Live Oak, maybe twenty feet high on a steep slope above the highway. We were still goofy from the short nap and couldn't think right. The four of us stood at the back of the engine, staring at the array of dials, gauges, and valves, wondering what to throw, what lines to pull. Exhaustion eats planning, understanding, and everything else. We needed to get the wet on the red, and we couldn't think it through. John lit a cigarette, which was a good move because I would then be the first to go in. Otherwise it would be me who'd look reluctant. Finally, the captain shook off the confusion and barked out "Drill one and drill three." It was a good call because it was simple and it got us moving.

It meant that I was to grab the live reel nozzle and take off. John would shoulder the hose pack, pull the large cotton jacketed hose with a "Y" fitting, and follow me. When I ran out of live reel, he would give me the hose pack, and I would set up one, maybe two, of the smaller lines. Then we could work both sides of the fire. Because we had to go into the overgrown arroyo to get to the base of the fire, the live reel would give us both protection and flexibility. I went in.

Despite the fact it was nearly midnight, the desert wind kept the temperature above at least eighty-five degrees, and the reflected heat was intense. The fire was working up the hill to my right and was spreading to a quarter-acre burn. The head of the fire up the hill was hot and my side started to heat up about thirty feet up. I hit everything at the foot of the fire with water, then started moving up my side. I climbed and hit it, climbed and hit it some more. And just when I was starting to knock it down, I ran out of hose.

Where was John? I dropped the nozzle and ran back down the line. At the bottom I found the "Y" set up, a shovel, and two hose packs. I dumped the rolled hose out of one of the packs and rigged to the "Y" so that John could take it up the other side of the fire. I shouldered the other pack and started back up my side of the line. In the dim light cast by the fire up the hill, I could make out two figures hunkered in the shelter of the live oaks at the foot of the burn. The captain was grinning, and John was throwing down a second cigarette, standing up, shaking his head and coming to help me. He looked pissed.

Later I found out why. It seems that after I took off with the live reel, John had gathered up the "Y" and pulled it behind him up the arroyo and to the foot of the fire. The captain had sent him back for hand tools and more hose packs. When John returned he found the captain squatting down and smoking at the base of the fire, watching my progress up the hill. John had joined him, hunkering down beside him and lit up a cigarette. He had just started telling a war story to pass the time and avoid climbing the hill when he stopped, sniffed, and asked the captain, "Hey, what smells so bad?"

He saw the captain's broad smile reflected in the light thrown by the fire, and finally noticed that the captain's pants were down. He was relieving himself in the dark. That was when I had arrived, and that's why John had lurched to his feet and thrown his smoke down in disgust.

The captain laughed. That's probably when he decided to give me that promotion.

Supervisory Verbatim #3

Addiction

Dr. Christopher Williams, Th.D. looked sternly at me. "Dr. Johnson, since you've decided to go ahead with both your trauma consultation and you're seeing me in a clinical supervisory capacity, I've been thinking more about your early experiences with the Forest Service."

"As have I," I ventured.

"Since you pay me, I'll go first," he said. "Last time we spoke, you told me about your experiences on that big forest fire above Santa Barbara."

"Almost *through* Santa Barbara. The Coyote Fire."

"Yes. And you have mentioned dreams relating to that fire and others. You talk of getting great joy out of being there, smelling the smoke, hearing the sounds associated with fire fighting."

"Ok."

"You mention an almost ecstatic pleasure."

"You're making it sound suspect," I said.

"Hear me out, please. You, yourself lecture about the body's emergency response, how it is a cascade of neurohormones like adrenaline."

"And others, the catecholamines to keep the reaction to adrenaline functional, and the endogenous opioids to blunt the pain and give a feeling of well being."

"Yes. The endogenous opioids. A powerful antidote to pain and suffering." He looked at me directly. "And isn't the flooding of endogenous opioids highly pleasurable? The result euphoric? And might not such a rush become addictive over time? So might we not wish to consider someone who goes off following sirens and fire trucks not just an adrenaline junkie, but perhaps also an opioid addict as well?"

"Yes, it certainly might," I admitted. I thought of how many times firefighters emerge coughing and wheezing after a firefight and immediately grab for a cigarette. The times I—having quite smoking for decades—would walk away from an intense session with a rescue team, and want that same cigarette.

The Bus Mechanic

Shit happens, granted; but some shit makes less sense than others. How do we make sense of the truly senseless? We look for resolution. Closure. We want things to wrap up in the end. Questions have to be answered. messes need to be cleaned up. It also helps if we can sort out the good guys from the bad because it feels good to assign praise and blame. It makes us think the world fits the way we think about it.

I'd spent half a career immersing myself in one critical incident after another and I needed to find a sense in it all. This incident seemed particularly pointless. Forty-five Girl Scouts with their seven adult leaders had boarded the chartered bus— one of a convoy of three—for the ride down the mountain overlooking Palm Springs following their Tramway excursion to the top of Mt. San Jacinto as part of their "California Dreamin'" Girl Scout tour of the Southland. The next stop on their tour would have been Disneyland. Following the accident, a photo of the group was published in the local newspaper. In the image, all the girls looked the appropriate mixture of excitement and nonchalance, the front row sitting in an arranged cheerleader pose. They sat there looking the way we all should look when we are that young, all fresh and wide-eyed.

They almost made it. The driver had managed to get the runaway bus down to the last serious curve when he had to dodge a van and a line of several slowly moving cars. The bus, with its forty-five Girl Scouts and seven leaders (all without seat belts), missed the turn, shot off the road, and rolled twice before colliding with several large boulders thirty feet down the hill. The impact was so great that the battered bus body separated from the chassis, twisted lengthwise. The front end and top were crushed, and the wheels splayed. There were bodies and personal effects strewn from the road down to the remains of the bus, tracing the path of the crash. Five Girls Scouts and two adults died at the scene. A sixth Girl Scout died later at one of the three area hospitals that received the injured.

The injured were treated by local medical personnel who responded without being asked. The rest of the girls and adults were taken to the Palm Springs Police Training Center to talk to their parents by phone, as the majority were from other parts of the country. Four were evidently from Finland.

I watch television personalities talk about how that the girls and their leaders described the accident:

> "An adult yelled at the driver to slow down."
> "The driver pumped the brakes frantically."
> "Headphones and radios fell to the floor."
> "A passenger slid into the aisle."
> "It felt like riding a roller coaster."
> "Someone yelled 'The brakes are out!'"
> "The bus driver saved a lot of people."

I read accounts of the adults involved:

> "I was just launched into the air."
> "Driver told someone 'Nothing's working!'"
> "Everything just went silent."
> "The sun was intense."
> "Young people lying everywhere."
> "It was very, very, very hot."
> "Adults laying in the wreck."
> "Can't remember how I got to the hospital."
> "There were some real heroes."

*   *   *

I read about heroes the next morning. An interesting set of news pieces appeared reporting that Palm Springs—playground of movie stars, golf champions, and politicos, and heartland of conspicuous consumption, nightclubs and poolside bikinis—responded in unexpected ways to the accident. Citizens donated blood. Hotels provided free rooms and meals to victims and promised rooms for their arriving families.

An ER trauma nurse was quoted as describing how Desert Hospital mobilized in minutes. One shift was just coming on duty, and those scheduled to go off shift stayed on. Gurneys lined the driveway. Everyone from medical staff to groundsmen, construction, janitorial, and maintenance people handled unloading the incoming injured. The chief surgeon described how doctors from all the surrounding communities arrived, whether or not they'd been formally requested. They worked for hours and triaged patients, beginning emergency treatment. Then they debriefed, regrouped, and planned the next steps.

At the time of the accident, Sonny Bono, the Mayor of Palm Springs, could have opted to watch newscasts from a safe perch in the air-conditioned city hall. He had plenty of opportunities there for leading press conferences and featuring in newscasts. Instead, he immediately called his wife Mary, told her about the accident, and then headed up the hill to the scene.

According to one personal interview, Mary got there and found Bono helping to carry a loaded stretcher up the hill from the overturned bus to the line of ambulances. One photo shows his face agonized, his shirt filthy and sweat-stained, as he labors to carry a girl whose head is bound to stabilize some set of fractures to her neck or spine. According to other interviews, Bono made many such trips up the steep hill putting stretchers in ambulances and into helicopters, and comforting the walking wounded. He had no special knowledge for this, no training. Another report quoted an emergency worker who said that Bono had to be shown how to approach a helicopter so he wouldn't be injured. Still, he kept on. Mary said it was a Sonny she had never seen before. Up until then, most of the public knew Sonny Bono as the somewhat diminutive half of the famed Sonny and Cher duo, as the mayor who rode up and down the main drag of Palm Springs on his motorcycle. The Sonny who wore paisley shirts and sported long hair and oversized glasses, now stood with blood on his work-shirt and pants. Even the lightweight moccasins were spattered. He had simply heard the call and immediately responded. He was weeping while Mary comforted him. She told a reporter that he said, "Mare, this is just horrible," that she believed that this had affected him more than any other event in his life. Sonny and Mary visited the girls in the hospital in the subsequent days until all survivors were released to their homes or their own hospitals.

*   *   *

But it wasn't Sonny I dealt with. I was called in by the bus company to consult with Phil, the mechanic who signed off on the bus. The National Transportation Safety Board investigation was still in full swing, but there were already news leak hints of brake adjustment problems. I visited the bus company maintenance garage, a dark, spacious bunker filled with quiet hulks of buses in states of disrepair. The garage was closed for business that day. I found Phil in his office chair, sitting quietly, emptying his desk into a cardboard box.

Phil was adamant that the brakes were good when he checked them. I expected him to say that; I may have been a neutral shrink, and certainly told him so, but how was he to know I wouldn't inadvertently pass on damning inside information in the middle of an ongoing investigation? Later I was to read the NTSB investigation report, and they did suggest the brake pedal assembly may have had more than optimal play, but it was a suggestive, not conclusive comment. Yet facts weren't Phil's main concern. The specter that he'd missed something that led to the deaths was bad enough, but old memories—

flashbacks and nightmares—triggered by the accident, were surfacing with a fury. There's no such thing as a simple bus mechanic—no more than a simple poet or a nuclear physicist. Like most people, this one had a story to tell.

Phil told me about a time long ago when he was an infantry sergeant in Korea. He'd been ordered to take his squad up one of those hills distinguished only by its number on an ordnance map and the fact that it had been reoccupied by the North Korean Army. He was to retake Hill #403. In the firefight that ensued, Phil and his squad took heavy losses. All of Phil's squad had been lost except for one who was pretty badly shot up. Medics were in short supply, so Phil slung the soldier over his shoulder and began the long climb down the hill under fire, threading between low lying brush and other disorganized troops.

Reaching the approach road Phil realized there was no field aid station set up yet and no apparent order to the company now in disarray. Still carrying his soldier he flagged down a passing tank, propped up the soldier on the tank's hull, then climbed aboard to hold him on as they rode back to the fire base to get medical aid.

Back at the fire base, halfway across the grounds, still carrying the unconscious bleeding boy he'd ordered up the hill, a sharp voice called, "Stop right there, soldier!" Phil turned to meet a fresh-faced junior officer obviously new to the field. The officer shouted, "You walked right by me and failed to salute!"

"Sorry, sir, I've got to get this man to medical." The man's blood was staining Phil's fatigues wicking down his legs and pooling in his boots.

"That's no excuse!" the officer bawled, warming to the task.

To speed things up, Phil tried reason: "Sir, there's a war on," he attempted.

"This is no war, soldier, this is a police action!"

Phil took a breath, shifted the injured man's weight to his other arm, then looked the officer in the eye. "If this is a police action, Sir, then I respectfully suggest you get up that god damned hill #403 and arrest those sons of bitches!"

In the ensuing flap that culminated over the court-martial, the fate of the bleeding soldier became lost in the paperwork.

I got Phil's inference, cynical as it was. If their god would allow Girl Scouts to die on the side of the road, the community couldn't be expected to be charitable. Phil wouldn't get a lot of sympathy from a lynch mob, nor their lawyers, searching for someone to blame, for something that was unthinkable, unacceptable. He figured the inevitable search for the guilty would soon pull into his mechanic's bay.

"Why don't you think you'll be exonerated in the investigation?" I asked Phil.

Phil sighed and stared out a window. "Cause you just can't leave 45 Girl Scouts dead and injured on a highway without burning a witch or two."

Helicopter Down

I wondered how I could help. My original Forest district had just called me back again to do an intervention with several fire engine crews who had just been involved with a helicopter crash, on a fire that was still burning near where we gathered. They had just been pulled off the line, fed, and brought in for the meeting. My job, as a therapist, was to give them a chance to talk about it and to see if anyone was showing signs of shock or distress, and share some pointers on how to take care of themselves. I set up for the group, made sure coffee was ready, and breathed the familiar smells of the District Office.

We filed around the large conference table in the main office and sat down. I introduced myself and set the ground rules for the discussion. They began to tell their stories.

All three engines had been regrouping on a large highway turnoff above a reservoir being used by helicopters to fill up their Bambi buckets that carried water slung under the ship. The helicopters flew water-dropping missions, attacking the fire in the canyons and hillsides above the reservoir. It was a hot day and the smoke hung low.

The engine task force was being regrouped and reassigned. As the crews awaited redeployment and lay on the top of the engine hose racks to rest, they watched the helicopters fly just over where they were parked, and tried to catch a cigarette and some shut-eye.

Hearing something wrong, they looked up to notice that one helicopter came out of the smokey canyon a little too low, too fast, just above them. As it pulled up, its skid caught the top power line and the line snapped, snaking up and wrapping itself around the skid. Like a kite on a string, the copter was pulled violently upward by centrifugal force, torqued backwards and over the power lines, and then hurtled down directly at the gathered engines below. The crews described hearing the commotion, seeing the helicopter's upward arc and their own leaping off the engines and scrambling underneath amid the wind, smoke, and noise as the helicopter fought momentum and gravity.

One described what followed: "I'd just scrambled under the engine and peered out from behind the big tires. The helicopter pilot was amazing; in the midst of the tumble, he somehow got the ship upright and put it into auto-rotate in time to slow the fall just enough so that when it hit—maybe twenty-five feet from where I lay—it managed to land upright on its skids." He shook his head and so did most of the rest of them. "It bounced hard but didn't explode. Sounded like the end of the world, but we're all still here and can talk about it. Things could have ended differently."

As the meeting drew to a close, I was approached by one of the younger firefighters, obviously new to his job. "Excuse me, sir. Is it always this . . . crazy around here?"

"Good question," I said. "I'd be asking that myself if I was new here." I was thinking about how I'd nearly been made crispy several times on my first year on this district. "This was extreme, and you had a right to be scared. It sounds like you did OK, though."

The young firefighter looked relieved.

Supervisory Verbatim #4

Flying Lessons

Walking past a small, rural airport, he noted the now familiar faded billboard with a small engine plane banking through some clouds. It read "Flying lessons: Inquire within." For the past year, whenever he saw the billboard he wondered what it would be like to fly. This time it was different. He turned up the drive leading to the airport. "Inquire within . . ."

Engine blasting rush
earth dropping away below;
gravity reconsidered.

* * *

"So that's it? That's how you, as a thirteen-year old kid, learned to fly airplanes?" asked Dr. Williams, cocking an eyebrow.

"That's pretty much how I started." I had to admit, it did seem improbable.

"Your parents signed the waiver? Paid for lessons?"

I wanted to fly. As a thirteen-year old boy I worked in a feed and fuel store five days a week after school. I'd endure loading bags of bird seed and dog food into open car trunks, shifting stock around, and the eternal sweeping and dusting in order to feed my love. I'd cash my check on Saturday morning and walk through the citrus groves and sage brush a couple of miles out to the local airport. There I would put my entire week's wages—minus enough for a Coke and Red Vines—down on a 30-minute flying lesson in an out-dated two person, stick-driven Aeronca L-16 or even just 15 minutes in a fancier Cessna 150. After the rush of take-off I would look down at the tiny houses, lemon groves, and cars below, amazed at the difference in perspective. It seemed like the drama of home and school, the tedium of life on the lemon grove, would all fall away.

"You learned to fly. How much?"

I told him how I learned to take off, orient in the sky, put the plane through basic maneuvers: turns, stalls, chandelles, and recovery from spins. I couldn't put into words the way the world looked from 3,000 feet. Or later, how it felt to be pulled off a burning mountain by a helicopter you were certain would crash. How Navy jets sounded when they took off and landed a hundred feet away from your head as you tried to sleep on a cot on the deck of a ship refueling at sea. How borate bombers made the earth shake when they dropped their load on your position on a fireline. How air attack pilots in the Forest Service were the last of the old west cowboys, and how debriefing them after a narrow escape was like sitting around a campfire spinning yarns.

I could tell him, though, how I had followed those aircraft into the mountains and across the seas as a shrink while I built my career working with emergency agencies. How I followed airplanes, helicopters, transports, fire engines, and ambulances into the heart of the biggest disasters and calamities of my time. Perhaps I hadn't described them in the grand detail I had remembered, because all he replied was one word.

"Why?"

"Why, what?"

"Why did you feel you had to do all of these things?"

"Well, they are exciting. I'm good at it."

"And," he pointed out simply, "you need the strokes. The spotlight. How much do you hunger for the affirmation your work brings?"

I was quiet.

Williams raised his hands in exasperation, "I feel like Daedalus,

the father of Icarus. The guy who built the wings so they could escape their island."

I was quiet.

"You're a bit like Icarus, here. Your daily practice, teaching and parenting stifle you; complacency seems to block your potential and you can't breathe. But your need for recognition and accomplishment drive you too high—crazy hours, extreme settings, a certain degree of personal risk. These bring you the affirmation for which you hunger. Like Icarus flying too high, though, you risk the sun melting the wax holding feathers on your wings. You risk tumbling out of the sky. The question is timing, I suppose. Can you get what you need and get out before the work robs you of your health, your family, and your peace of mind?"

Firestorm

A wind shear had knocked down most of the trees on the lee slope of the mountain, and so far only the trunks had been salvaged. Branches and duff lay several feet thick and had dried brittle hard after two years of drought. Terpene fumes rose from the piles of needles and resin-rich pine kindling. When the huge fire finally came over the back of the mountain, it showered sparks along the entire slope. A thousand little starts joined one another and soon the entire mountain went up in a firestorm that resembled those solar flares that twist across the face of the sun.

The firestorm followed its own convection across the bottom of the canyon, barely pausing to eat a set of cabins as it passed. It seems that two engine companies on scene saw the circle of eight cabins, each pair with a large propane tank between them. Knowing it could be hot, the two captains decided to drop off their crews in a safe area then return to the cabins alone. They parked the engines side by side, laid out hose, engaged their pumps, and were putting wet to red when the firestorm hit. Flames swirled over and around, and engulfed the cabins in seconds. Searing winds evaporated water before it could reach from the engines to the cabins. One of the captains said that it was so hot that the cabins seemed to be shimmering. The propane tanks were beginning to cook-off, and the pressure relief valves sounded like jets. The two captains took refuge in one of the cabins, certain they were dead.

Later, in the debriefing, I asked them what they did in the few minutes they had in that cabin. "We found beers in the refrigerator and had one. We wrote last messages to our families and closed them up in the refrigerator, figuring the letters might outlast us and be found later. Then, after we finished the beers, we decided this was not how we wanted to die. We wanted to go down fighting. We went back out into the firestorm, fired up the engines and pumps. We shot water into the wall of flame, into structures that were fully involved even though it was pointless. It was just a relief to be doing something rather than nothing."

"So how did you make it out?"

"It was weird," one said. "All of a sudden, there was a break. We could see a spot of blue through the fire. We threw down our nozzles and ran through the ring of cabins toward the periphery. We dove through and kept rolling till we were clear. We were just lucky."

At this point in the debriefing, their crews, who had been sitting together listening to this, all stood up and pressed forward with tears running through the ashes on their faces to embrace their captains. They held each other and wept.

Supervisory Verbatim #5

After Markleeville

Dr. Williams saw me a month after I'd returned from Markleeville, and he was looking concerned. "How are you feeling?" he asked.

"All right, I guess."

"Meaning you're fine, or meaning you don't know how to begin," he coaxed.

"Meaning more less Ok, but I'm tired."

"Sleeping alright?"

"Pretty much, but I'm having a lot of bad dreams."

He probed further. "A lot of different bad dreams or the same one?"

"Different versions of the same dream. I find myself on emergency incidents, and then I'm just not sure what to do. I feel like I ought to know what to do, but I don't."

"Not so good in your line of work?"

"I feel like I should."

"Tell me about one of the dreams that you can remember," Dr. Williams.

"Ok," I started. "Here's the one from last night. I find myself in a big Class I Incident Command,"

"Hold it," he interrupts. "A what?"

"There are different sizes of incidents. The biggest, Class I, are the most complicated with divisions. The command center has a set of trailers or tents. In my dream, I was walking among tents, but didn't know why."

"Go on," he prompted again.

"So I get hit with a set of important realizations, one at a time, with stuff going on in between. First, I realize I'm supposed to be here, even though I have no idea even what kind of incident it is. So I set out to find the Plans tent, because they'd have a map and some situation reports I could look at. On my way I pass some emergency people who are avoiding eye contact, and I come to realize that I don't know what my role here is. Am I a consulting shrink, a firefighter, or something else?

"Then another realization: I might even be the Operations Chief. An O.C. who doesn't even know what kind of incident it is, much less what to do about it. Another crew passes and they are looking at me and grinning. They know I'm a fraud. Then I realize that everybody there knows, and they also know that my being there, my not knowing anything, is intentional—part of some kind of plan. I'm meant to be there, not knowing anything! And just at that moment everything in the dream shifts. Fire is blowing into the Incident Command, tents are burning, crews are running around, just like it happened on one of the big fires I was on."

Dr. Williams signals me to keep going. "But then all my confusion and indecision is over. I see one of the engines careening by and jump on the running board and order the driver toward a burning tent and holler 'You! Put the wet on the red!'. Once I know what's going down, it becomes obvious what to do. I woke up in a full sweat."

Dr. Williams did not look so confused.

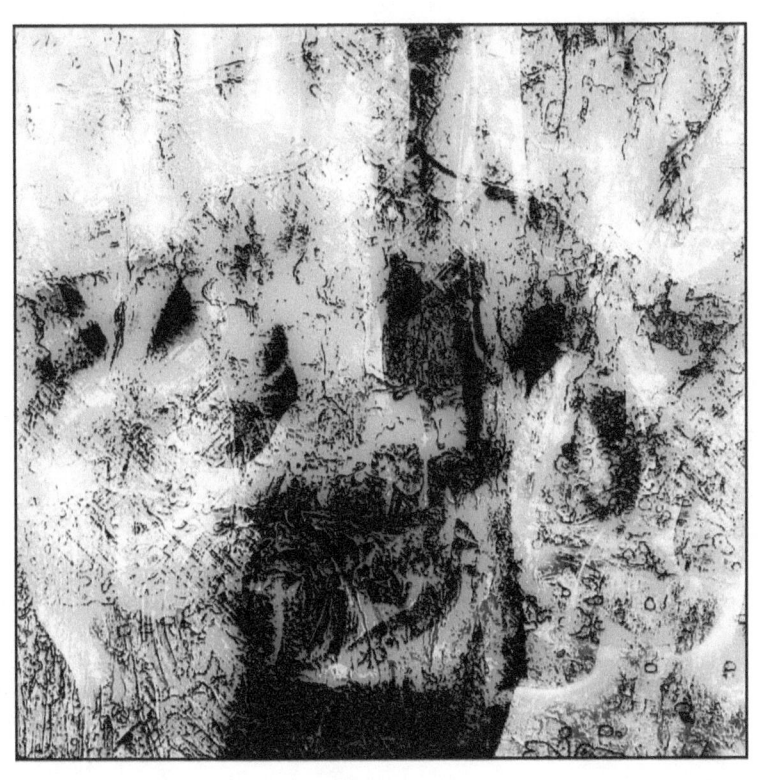

PART II

INCIDENTS AND TANGLES

Two terms have become familiar in common parlance, both originating in the Army during World War II and richly described by Bill Mauldin, *Stars and Stripes* cartoonist laureate and apologist for the common dogface foot soldier, in his book, *Up Front*: SNAFU and FUBAR. The former describes the normalcy of abnormal situations—Situation Normal, All Fucked Up. Inadequate supplies (and flooding of inappropriate supplies), communication tangles, unintelligible intelligence, and impossible physical and mental demands in disaster situations are to be expected in the field. These are normal in the field in wartime and during natural and human-origin disaster. FUBAR, on the other hand, is when things become so messed up that they are unbelievable—Fucked Up Beyond All Recognition. That's usually when the commanders would call in a field shrink. I was called in at the height of the Yellowstone Fire Complex in 1988. The promised helicopter transport from the airport in Billings, Montana to the Incident Command of one of the biggest fires was grounded by smoke. I had to join a convoy that climbed over two passes to get in. Upon arrival, I was escorted through the command center. My escort knocked on the commander's tent flap. A minute later the commander threw back the flap and emerged. He was unkempt, of course, with messy clothes and hair, a several-weeks-old beard and swollen eyes. Standing there in lantern light, he blinked through smudged face, looked at me, and said, "Thank God you're here." With a good part of the state burning, towns nearly engulfed, and half of the National Interagency Class I Incident Commands deployed here, I was sorely tempted to reply that, if that were the case, we were all in a world of hurt. That was a FUBAR situation. It would not be my last.

By this time things were heating up in my private practice, too. The images I carried around in my head multiplied logarithmically both in number and in kind. The simple "if this happens, then do that" protocols of my training could not keep up with the multi-factored judgements I had to make in the field, where limited resources, complex needs, and rapidly unfolding situations often required best-guess decisions resulting in consequential actions made under trying conditions. If you aren't improvising when things go FUBAR you're not doing your job.

Not only that, my willingness to accept difficult assignments and make assessments of complex situations became impacted by my own personal background. Intense memories of firefighting and Vietnam situations sometimes emerged unbidden and affected my judgements. I often relied on my advisor, clinical supervisor Christopher Williams, Th.D. to help me find my way through these thickets of my own making. It helped that he was former US Air Force as well as an Episcopal Priest. I secretly wondered if I, myself, was going FUBAR.

Evensong

Leaden sky through thicker windows high above cross shaped floor, Anglican following Catholic form. Tourists join faithful, queued up for Evensong at Westminster Abbey, filing in behind the ministerial host and filling up the designated choir seats less than 100 feet from where Coronations of English Kings and Queens have been performed for centuries.

*   *   *

My flight landed at 6 a.m. Heathrow time. Day was breaking nine hours prematurely. My body said it was only sundown. Elizabeth was waiting for me at baggage claim as she'd promised.

"Let's gather your bags. I'm making a proper English breakfast for you at my house. Richard will be up by then. We've found some nice Cumberland sausage, and the tomatoes have just ripened."

Hurtling down the wrong side of the road against London traffic added to my disorientation.

"You wouldn't mind a brief stop on the way, would you? Our local newspaper reporter would like to know something of why you're here. I thought it would be perfect promotion for your talks. Just a few minutes."

She'd flown in a year ago to listen to me speak in New York and was now paying for this excursion.

"Not at all," I mumbled.

*   *   *

The choir faces itself and the rest of us beneath reading lamps that are a suitable dark red. The deeply worn stones carry the patina of countless steps, trod upon by those who bear witness to communion.

We stopped at the newspaper office in Newbury, parking in front. William Symonds motioned us into his cramped cubicle and waved us into chairs beside a desk in disarray. Clippings, pages of notes, and folders competed with a computer screen that pulled Symonds' glance every few seconds. "So, Dr. Johnson, what brings you to the U.K.?"

*   *   *

Red shades illuminating choir boy and girl faces and the adult choir members behind them. Locals and tourists alike fill in the choir pews beside those singing; soft creaks and pops as the pews adjust to shifting weight. Fading light outside the high stained glass windows adds quiet light to the glow within.

I outlined how I'd been asked to speak to a number of groups about children's reactions to trauma and ways to help them cope. How The Centre for Crisis Management and Education—Elizabeth's outfit—had organized speaking engagements with Red Cross teams in Oxford, inner-city teachers in London, and with military and rescuers in Surrey.

"About what?" Symonds asked.

"Trauma." She pronounced it 'traumar.' "You know, Bill; startle reactions, anxiety, nightmares, that sort of thing. We spoke of this. Like the Ferry disaster you covered where so many students on that field trip drowned. Like that house fire in town that burned the family. Like Albania."

"Albania?" I asked.

Symonds looked away for a moment and then back at me. "I covered the civil war in 1997. Never got over it, I suppose. Still dream of the orphanage in Tirana with all those pale children lying in beds lined up against the wall. Nurses wouldn't hold them because it hurt too much. Hearing about the executions. Untreated mutilations from the fighting."

He stared at his computer screen, but he was seeing something else—scenes of suffering seared into his memory—something far away.

"Did you have anyone to talk to about it when you got back?"

"Elizabeth," Symonds replied, nodding at her. "But I guess I wasn't ready to talk. It was all a bit of a blur at the time." Bill went on to recount images of war and mayhem, one after another. He'd been sent to follow the stories; if it bleeds it leads. An hour, and several lifetimes later we emerged from the office.

"Sorry about that," Elizabeth muttered to me on our way to her car. "I suppose poor Bill doesn't get much of a chance to talk about it." Two hours in-country and I'm already exhausted.

Some notes from that day:
> Hungerford

Red Cross
> Croatia
> (Ginny's pers)
>> Mau Mau (?)
> MV Jupiter
> Suicide
>> (another day here?)

Bath
> rejection by Society

to Manor (girl cartwheeling through air—
> (limbs separating)
>> 4 hour siege

torture cellar
> man on fire, Bradford

But not much of my notes make sense. I'm having trouble keeping it all sorted.

*　　*　　*

Angel voices rise
history palpates, disbelief suspended.
Ascension while waiting here
standing over Darwin's bones.

St. Hilda's College, Oxford. The knock came at nearly half past eleven, just enough time for me to have just fallen asleep after a long day of lecture. Nigel stood in my doorway. He was with the Red Cross, retired from a middle-management position in the sanitation department and was now running the local Red Cross agency. "I'm sorry to bother you this late, Doctor, but some things you said today brought up memories."

I invited Nigel into my dorm room and rounded up a drink for the two of us. Nigel spent the next hour or so talking about incidents he'd been involved in while serving in his current position. It took a long time for Nigel to tell me about his involvement in the Herald of Free Enterprise Ferry disaster. The one that involved dead children.

The proverbial British stiff upper lip seems to loosen when a sympathetic ear arrives from out of town.

*   *   *

'I found I'd been left in a field of bones. Many bones lay about and were dry. My Lord said to me: "Prophecy these bones" and I did. And as I did so there came a noise, a rattling, and the bones knit together and grew flesh. I breathed upon them, and the breath came into them and they stood.' Adapted from Ezekiel 37: 1-14

*   *   *

As early as A.D. 639—in the early Medieval period—gifts or acknowledgements of ownership of land were recorded in charters. These were usually written on parchment in Latin, sometimes in the vernacular. A Saxon Charter from A.D. 934 mentions a forest in a tract of land now called Savernake, near

Marlborough in Berkshire County. The forest is now protected land, covered in beech and oak. Some of the notable trees are affectionately named with monikers like "King of Limbs," or "Big Belly." Susan Godfrey, a mother of two young children, came to picnic in this sylvan forest on August 19, 1987. At 12:30 p.m. she was shot dead for no apparent reason.

After shooting Susan Godrey to death, Michael Ryan, a 27-year-old antique dealer, stopped for petrol at the Dean's of Froxfield station on the A4. He was on his way back to his row house in Huntington, a medium-sized town in Berkshire County, where he lived with his mother. He picked up a few things from the station shoppe, filled a five-gallon can of petrol, and put it in the boot of his car. Then Ryan pulled out an automatic rifle and went back into the station where he shot at the attendant, missing her. He drove on to his mother's house, shot and killed her, then reloaded the weapon, slung bandoliers of additional rounds of bullets over his shoulders, and put several pistols with extra rounds into his pockets. He then sloshed gasoline around the inside of his mother's row house before he tossed a match and went out the back door. There he noticed a neighbor, an older pensioner, coming out of the back door several houses down. He shot and killed the neighbor over the fence and entered the house and murdered that neighbor's wife. Ryan then proceeded to work his way through Hungerford, shooting anyone he came across.

* * *

Agnus Dei,

she pulls her evening scarf close
wonders if it's time to leave the priesthood
thinks about her son's tuition

qui tollis peccata mundi,

she wants to sit down
she holds her umbrella comfortably close
she wonders if the priest wanders

dona nobis pacem.

*　　*　　*

The local police were unarmed and the county Special Weapons and Tactics team was out of the county, in London, participating in a training. Without them, the Hungerford constabulary was unable to do more than attempt to direct traffic away from the shooting and attend to the wounded. Ryan was moving so quickly and erratically, however, that traffic was inadvertently directed into harm's way as often as away. Carloads of locals and tourists drove right into the carnage.

By the time the SWAT team had returned, Michael Ryan had killed sixteen people and wounded fifteen others. Running out of ammunition, he took refuge in the John O'Gaunt Secondary School (named after John O'Gaunt, Duke of Lancaster, son of Edward III, uncle of Richard II, and father of Henry the IV)—where Ryan used to go, and eventually took his own life.

While several medical doctors and psychiatrists and journalists have weighed in on possible causes for the mass shooting and with diagnoses for Ryan, a local vicar was quoted as saying ". . . it is not something that can be explained."

*　　*　　*

> "We have sinned against you and against our neighbor, in thought, word, and deed. Through negligence, through weakness, and through our own deliberate fault . . ."

*　　*　　*

On the way back from Hungerford, Elizabeth pulled up alongside a school playing field and pointed to a modest roadside marker with a small plaque. "They just put it in last month."

"What's it about?"

"In 1943 an errant German bomber pilot, thinking he was over his London target, released his bombs too early. One landed here. It was just at recess and the schoolchildren were out to play. His bomb killed most of the village children."

"And this is the commemoration? What was the ceremony like?"

"It was the fifty year anniversary last month," Elizabeth replied. "The vicar said a few words, but only a handful of people came to the gathering. They stood under their umbrellas in the rain and then left when the vicar finished.

"Nobody in the village had spoken aloud about it for fifty years."

*   *   *

Priest: *O Lord, shew thy mercy upon us.*
Answer: *And grant us thy salvation.*
Priest: *O Lord, save the Queen.*
Answer.   *And mercifully hear us when we call upon thee.*

*   *   *

The British find comfort in ritual, sometimes bordering on what others may find inane. At six in the morning of the first day of May in Oxford, thousands of students, faculty, townspeople, and visitors gather under the high Magdalen College tower to listen to the choir sing the *Hymnus Eucharisticus*. Following the music, the celebrants, many having celebrated all night before, engage in singing, feasting, and jumping off the Magdalen Bridge into the cold waters of the River Cherwell below.

*   *   *

Lighten our darkness, we beseech thee, O Lord; and by thy great mercy defend us from all perils and dangers of this night...

*   *   *

We stopped and had lunch and a pint in a pub outside Heathrow before my flight. A local told us about how he, when he worked for British Petroleum in Nigeria, had been kidnapped and tortured for ransom three months ago. He was recuperating before going back.

*   *   *

The grace of our Lord Jesus Christ, and the love of God, and the fellowship of the Holy Ghost, be with us all evermore. Amen. —From the Book of 2 Corinthians 13.[ii]

---

ii   Service text from *The Book of Common Prayer*, the rights in which are vested in the Crown, is reproduced by permission of the Crown's Patentee, Cambridge University Press.

Layers

"So tell me about the shooting?" I asked the team. That was what the team leader had told me was the reason I'd been asked to provide an advanced crisis team training. We sat in the cafeteria of the elementary school—once in the suburbs; now it felt like inner-city. This northern industrial state had fallen to financial misfortune, and this city suffered the worst.

A single shooting. The team had formed several years ago, the leader said, and had been pressed into service a lot. Now they'd run into something that had challenged them beyond their comfort zone. One of their students had been shot and killed. Usually that wasn't enough to drag me halfway across the country. There had been something about the initial telephone conversation that interested me. I wanted to know more.

The crisis team training had gone well so far. Several teams from other schools had been invited to join the training in order to allow a regional coordination in case of community disaster. The expanded group had been attentive through the first day, asked questions and discussed issues helpfully. We'd moved quickly through the review of basics. I was looking forward to getting past the group debriefing and on to strategic planning.

Now we were setting up the debriefing simulation, and I'd invited the original team that had undergone the shooting to be a demonstration group I'd debrief in front of the others. They bobbed their heads up and down and looked enthusiastic at the prospect. The other invited teams would sit around the outside of the group and observe the process first-hand. I'd ridden this rodeo several times before. The only difference between this and a real debriefing was the depth we'd go. We'd keep it light. Or so I thought.

We'd gone through the initial stages of introductions, rule settings, times, and circumstance. Now we brought up the incident. Various team members took turns filling out the story. It kept getting worse. As I'd been briefed, there had been a shooting. It turned out that the shooting had taken place on campus, on the playground. A girl had been shot.

While I wasn't callous to their situation, I guessed it was more involved than that. "So a girl was shot?"

Another spoke up, "She was well-liked. And she was only five years old."

"A kindergartner? Oh, man . . ."

"Yes," another answered. "and she was shot on the playground. In front of the recess crowd."

"So there were a large number of witnesses to deal with— other children, adults?"

"There's more," George, a psychologist on the team added. "She was shot with a shotgun."

"Oh, dear," I said. "That sounds really bad. With a shotgun it would have been more ugly. It probably couldn't get uglier."

"Yes, it was uglier," the team leader said, looking down. "The shooter was her own ten year old sister."

The silence in the room was heavy. It was much heavier than I had planned to go with this training simulation. Now we were going to have to be more thorough, get into more feelings and reactions that the team might be comfortable sharing in front of their colleagues from the other schools.

But this group was special. They wanted to talk about the incident and so they soldiered on. For another half hour we kept going. We talked about how they operated as a team, what they did with the situation, how they felt about it at the time, we talked about their reactions afterward. I was about to launch into the part about how they could take care of themselves in the future when one of the team gave voice to something I hadn't anticipated.

"The problem we're having isn't this particular incident," the school counselor said. "It's deeper than that. We get an incident like this on the average of once every few weeks. And every week there's a smaller incident or two or three. It's unending."

An older gentleman said, "Most of us signed on to work here when it was a different place. There were two big factories in town, and they employed most of the people who lived in this neighborhood. This used to be a school of kids who came from middle class families who valued education and supported what we did. We had been trained to focus on academics and healthy kids."

"When the factories closed, the families had to move. So many that the banks were foreclosing on most of the houses, and the neighborhood was nearly vacant. They couldn't sell the houses. Then the squatters started moving in. What used to be a solid neighborhood turned into shooting galleries, gang havens, poverty, drugs, violence. The police stayed out when they could, ambulances became the primary health care provider, and we became the main social agency. We weren't trained for that. We're now into our third year of this apocalypse."

The training had shifted gears. We talked about how the conditions of their work was affecting them on a personal level. We brought up things that normally aren't discussed in trainings, or in debriefings. They told me about how they were becoming isolated—from their colleagues, their families, and themselves. "Dr. Johnson," one stated, "I just don't know who I am anymore."

Another pointed out how the values that had led her to teaching now seemed far away. "I'm doing things I never thought I'd do, passing students from my class that should have failed, just so they'd be gone. Closing my heart to these students." One man pointed out that he knew other teachers who carried handguns. "I'm not saying I carry, but I sure understand why they might." Another: "I came here to teach. Now I come to get my check, and I want to get the hell home in one piece. But that's not really who I am. I'm becoming someone I don't know any more and I don't respect or like."

How could this possibly end positively, I wondered. It would take more than band-aids and simplistic answers. We worked at writing personal plans for dealing with the central hurts and pain. It seemed so little compared to the enormous challenges they faced as a team and as individuals at that school with all its soul-numbing tribulation. Yet at the day's end there was applause and a line formed to shake hands and give hugs. Most important, they held each other. "Thank you for coming this far," one said to me. "We didn't know if you would make it."

Supervisory Verbatim #6

Under Layers

A little while after I got back from giving my last training in Flint, I met with my clinical supervisor Dr. Williams as I usually do following big incidents. I settled into my favorite chair. After my initial description of events, he seemed to be sizing me up. "So as I understand it," Williams began, "you walked into more than you had bargained for."

"In a sense. I hadn't been given the whole story going in. I don't know whether it was because they intentionally withheld information, or whether the person who invited me really didn't have a sense of it herself. In any case, it was less an ambush than an unexpected opportunity."

"How so?" he asked.

"I got a chance to uncover—or at least articulate—something I'd been trying to make sense of for some time." Williams looked at me questioningly. I pushed on. "How sustained exposure to traumatic stress—low-level like in counseling or high-level like in combat—affects people differently than single incident stress."

"And why on earth would you want to go there?"

"Because it would shift how we'd do things like debriefings or incident consultation. We'd be better able to address central issues."

Williams held me in his clinical gaze, "So what did you learn from these folks? And how did you learn it?"

I welcomed the chance to talk about what I did. "I shifted the nature of the various stages of our conversation. In a regular debriefing we talk about what we saw and heard, then we talk about our reactions at the time and shortly afterwards, then our lasting symptoms."

"Standard debriefing." I didn't realize yet that he had a different agenda.

"Right. But I realized that was missing something important, so I changed it up—fishing, maybe, but their faces looked like they had more to say if I was to understand them. This time, we went through the different kinds of incidents that their team had been hit with over the past 18 months. We listed changes that had occurred in their thinking and feelings over the 18 months. Rather than all the details, we looked for highlights, the things that stood out in their memory."

Williams still looked interested. "Must have taken a while. Exhausting, I imagine."

Noticing the darkening of his eyes I wondered if I'd missed something. "The whole thing probably took a couple of hours," I continued. "Then we looked at the most important of their emotional reactions in key incidents or in between incidents. It was when we got into the long-range reactions that things got interesting."

"Do you mean the nature of the reactions?"

"Very much so. While I wrote the things they talked about up on the board, pretty soon the different reactions began to cluster. I ended up re-sorting and consolidating into four basic groups. These people were wearing out, running out of gas. But in specific ways. They all tended to be losing their sense of purpose, both personally and in their work. They felt they were losing their connection with others, particularly their families."

"Fascinating," he pointed out. "So this is more than your standard anxiety and depression, it's more than post-trauma, but it isn't full blown psychosis."

"Right. You expect some of these reactions in depression, but not in such a specific pattern."

"Huh . . ." He was quiet for a minute.

I still thought he was dazzled by my breakthrough. "Yeah. Sometime I'll show you an informal assessment tool I've developed from it. I've used it with a couple of different groups and it's amazing how it can guide the consultation. Gives a clear pattern and sets the direction for work."

"What do you think you'll do with it?"

Not seeing where he was going, I elaborated. "I've been doing some work with Harlem Hospital on another project. I'm going to be in Buffalo at a conference in February. Maybe I'll talk to the Harlem people about it."

He smiled. "They'll probably be interested. In the meantime, perhaps, maybe we should talk about the results some more."

"How so?"

"I'm wondering how this conversation fits you, how your repeated exposure to traumatic events is affecting you—how would you answer your little questionnaire? Do you think maybe what you're doing could be getting in the way of who you are, or might your independence be affecting your family? Let me pose a little thought-experiment; if these were ways to measure spirituality, then do you work in a cathedral every day, or are you beginning to wander alone in the desert?"

Evacuation

The fire progressed steadily through the tall pines up the long valley in the Sawtooth Mountains north of Boise. All but one of the cabins had been evacuated. Fire crews were attempting to protect structures, but also fighting a rear-guard action in the face of the advance. I had been sent to talk the old man out of his cabin before he was cooked. "He'll burn. Just see if you can get him out of there," the IC had said.

I knocked on his door. He opened, squinting against the amber light and stinging smoke. "Mr. Bartlett? I'm Doc Johnson. The Incident Commander asked me to come by and talk to you."

"Who are you?"

"Doc Johnson. I'm the fire shrink. They have me work with the firefighters, usually."

"And old farts like me," he smiled a little. "I'm Ted Bartlett. Glad to meet you. I don't need to be shrunk."

I couldn't help smiling. Two engines went by making hearing difficult. "Mind if I come in?"

"Suit yourself. I got water."

We sat in the living area of the small place, decorated with stuffed deer heads and hand-mounted posters from old *Outdoor Life* and *Field and Stream* magazines. Lanterns, saws, and Indian blankets hung on the walls. An oil cloth draped the small table as a gesture toward civility. We drank our water.

"So what are you supposed to say," he inquired patiently.

"I'm supposed to ask you to leave, Mr. Bartlett, to evacuate with the rest of the cabin owners." I looked beyond him out the window, from which I could see the approaching glow from the flames. I heard one of the engines backing up to the cabin.

"There's no way they can save this place."

"Well, that's kind of you, and the Incident Commander. But you shouldn't have bothered. I'm not leaving."

I sipped my water. "Why not, if you don't mind my asking?"

"No, I don't mind. I've had this place all my life. It was my family's summer cabin until they passed, it's my year-round home now." He looked around. "It's what I know."

I thought about that. "You don't have family?"

"Not here, anyway. And they don't want me there."

"Out of contact?"

"Pretty much," he allowed. "We fell out a few years ago. Couldn't seem to get it back together."

The red glow was getting brighter, hotter. The wind was picking up, and I heard something hit the roof.

"So you're telling me that if you left here, you'd pretty much have no place to go."

Then something hit the window. I looked up and saw a frothy pink foam being sprayed on the outside walls. This meant the crew was about to give up on the cabin, insulate it, and move on. They'd officially thrown in the towel.

"Look, Mr. Bartlett," I began.

"Ted . . ." he interrupted.

"Look, Ted. These guys outside, me, we've got to live for years with what you are about to do. Marshall law has not been declared. We legally cannot pull you out of here. You will burn to death, and we'll be left with that. You'll haunt us for years. Please do not do that to us."

He was quiet for a long time. I could hear the snapping and the groan of the approaching fire. The red was beginning to peek through the pink foam through the window. I could smell the smoke.

Ted sighed and looked around his home. "You're right, Doc. You can't live with that. I can't die with it, either. I guess we'd better go."

He got up from his chair and we headed for the door. I noticed he already had his bag packed.

Supervisory Verbatim #7

Vietnam

We had to meet on the Fourth of July since I was going to be gone during our normal appointment time the next day. I sat down across from Dr. Williams. "I appreciate your meeting on the Fourth. It's a holiday and you shouldn't have to work."

"I don't have to work," he replied, I chose to."

"You don't like the Fourth? The hot dogs and fireworks?"

He smiled, "Overdone. I don't like all the posturing and folderol. I was in the Air Force during Korea. And I notice it's the Fourth and *you're* here."

My turn to smile, "Yeah. I've got mixed feelings about the day. Growing up, I was on the city fireworks crew. My father and his best friend started the celebration in town. Nepotism; I got promoted. I used to love being on the mortar crew and firing."

"But, . . ."

"Too many associations," I said.

"Hmm." He waited. "Vietnam? Maybe we should talk about that and see how it might be affecting your work."

"Yeah," I nodded. "Probably should."

Supervisory Verbatim #8

O'Brien's Choice

"So what's this business about O'Brien? Who is he?" asked Dr. Williams.

"A writer. He wrote a story about deciding whether or not to let himself get drafted into Vietnam." I replied.

"What brings this up; why now?"

"I met the guy. I always liked his writing. Then I heard he was going to be signing at a bookstore near here. There he was in the coffee shop next door to the bookstore, and he graciously spoke to me while we waited for his time to speak at the signing. I wanted to talk about a scene in one of his books where an older friend rowed him across the Canadian border by boat, ostensibly fishing."

"Oh?"

"Yeah," I continued. "The main character was contemplating dodging the draft, and suddenly he had to choose to go or not to go to war. All he had to do was slip over the side and swim to peace."

"Hmmm," muttered Dr. Williams. "What happened?"

"He anguished, sitting there in that boat—years of contradictory conditioning came down to a life-shaping choice. The decision cost him thirteen months and a wake-up, followed by nearly thirty years wondering why he hadn't run."

"So he didn't go over the side? Once again," Williams pressed, "why this, and why now?"

"I made a similar decision. Some people found it easy. I didn't."

"You decided to go too?" he asked

"Yeah. It wasn't easy at the time, and it's never gotten easier. Lousy warrior, lousy pacifist. Back in those middle-1960 days, I sat in a similar boat, listening to protest music, traveling with the international student set, holding heated political discussions into the night. But there was this other side, you know? For some reason unknown to me, I was always pushing some envelope. I just had to drop out of school. Just had to fight wildfires with the forest service. Had to drink in bad bars. Had to climb mountains. Here's a question: when a young man is obsessed with proving himself, exactly what is it he is trying to prove?"

"You tell me," Dr. Williams said.

"I don't know, maybe it's more about what he wants to prove he *isn't*. What unspeakable doubts to have. How much evidence of his own adequacy, strength, goodness, and capability would it take to set the questions to rest?"

Dr. Williams didn't say anything.

"It's easier to see now. I've been amused at the antics of my friends and neighbors, the sudden outbreak of American flags flying defiantly on their Expeditions, Cherokees, and other suburban assault vehicles as they careen about. They look like the images we see in news reports of pickup trucks careening through Kabul and Baghdad, loaded with armed militiamen. The best story I've heard was about the guys down the street who, armed with deer rifles and shotguns, had piled out of their houses at 6:30 on September 11 and stood around in the dawn's early light, standing guard against marauding Afghanis. I think about the Gulf of Tonkin Resolution and wonder just how south things can go. Last week I sent a paper off to a journal about the school's response to terrorism. It may already be dated. The Feds are leaking conversation about "dirty bombs," radioactive material packed in conventional explosives. It seems the Russians have been selling a lot of it to pay for the difference between communism and The Good Life."

Dr. Williams waited for me to reach a point, and I finally arrived:

"Here's my main worry: maybe I don't pack the gear anymore. My head says it's mass confusion back there. My heart says be patient. So do my friends. My stomach, on the other hand, feels the grip. Lately, I'm beginning to think that the universe has figured me out. Something inside hasn't been ready. Have I been reassigned to O'Brien's Boat? Am I again sitting here looking at the beach, feeling my legs turn to lead?"

"So, you've faced this business before, feeling fear."

"One summer night before enlisting, I spoke with my father about these things, at least indirectly. By 1965 we were talking again, albeit mostly by letters—my mother would remark about how odd it was to see two grown men sidle up to one another and then just pass off a crumpled envelope. We mostly spoke then of the Big Questions, and the growing conflict in Southeast Asia certainly qualified. My cousin was already there, a First Officer on a gunboat, and another was fixing to leave as an Air Traffic Controller for the Army at Pleiku. Dad served with the Army in the Battle of the Bulge during the Big One, and I obsessed about the political and moral dimensions of this one.

"It wasn't easy for me to approach him. Finally, I screwed up my nerve and threw out the opener; 'When you were over there, didn't you ever find yourself appalled by the evil of war?'

"Understand—my old man was neither a stupid nor shallow man. And, in retrospect, he probably was thanking his God that he had a chance to speak the unspeakable with his kid, whether or not he could say anything sensible. 'I dunno,' he pulled at his professorial beard for a while, as if trying to milk something helpful out of it. 'I was pretty young at the time, I guess. It wasn't so much good or bad, for me. It was just big, mostly. Big.'"

4 July, 1967.

A guy comes back from Vietnam, right? Freshly back from destroyer duty, from months of nights of firing, days of interdiction, from slowly eroding sanity and self—as luck would have it—on the Fourth of July. Not just anyone's Fourth, you understand. Not just the crêpe paper bicycles, small town parade, and booths in the park. You have to understand the community here.

My family has three generations on the city fireworks crew. I inherited the mortar boss job from my father; directing twelve people firing mortars by hand, working all day before, and half that night cleaning up. Hard, dirty work shoveling brick dust, sorting shells, and building frames as the hot California sun went down. Arranging mortar shells in firing order in the tarp covered "kitchen" where they'd be safe from sparks. Setting the tubes for the just-right arc to send firepower into that dark sky. Looking down on mere civilians who knew nothing of the acrid burn of fuse, about struggling for breath or about the unearthly light. They didn't fear hang fires, short fuses, and shorter fingers. They'd never touch that archetypal power and hope to merge with it all.

Now back from the real thing where the rocket's red glare meant killing some and saving others, where some of those you saved would kill again, where hate was in season and it really wasn't all that symbolic or romantic or right. About these things, the civilians still knew nothing and seemed to care less. Nor did most of the fireworks crew. Nor did I, really, not anymore. Who there on that field, listening to the Sousa band and watching the mortars and mine-bags and bombs, knew? Who knew how it had been and still was for those still there? Not these people gathering in the stands that night to sing patriotic songs. And certainly not those whom I loved.

But there in the gathering gloom, I had darker fantasies. Hordes of war protestors would march down 6th Street to overturn our mortar tubes, destroy our show, and lay waste to our Fourth of July. I would turn the mortars on those who would spit and call me "baby-killer," those who would invite chaos to supper, those who would tear down our carefully-maintained charade of order. I would turn the mortars on those who would tell the truth.

But when it was show time and everything started, the show boss wouldn't let me fire.

"Just wasn't sure," he would explain later, "just back, and all. A little crazy." Asshole, I thought.

What the fuck does he know about crazy? Right? "You tell me just what the fuck is crazy," I yelled back at him. He'd never pulled the trigger. He walked away, leaving me standing there in the dark trying to get my fists to unclench.

So I just leaned against the car near the kitchen on that hot, July night and watched the show. I was feeling out of place, thinking about the ship, wondering if it had been hit by rocket fire from the shore yet. They had a hang-fire half way through the opening. It was one of those mortar shells that explodes into a bunch of mini-rockets that shoot back and fourth, shrieking and changing directions chaotically. When the sparks whistled in close and everybody cheered, I dove under that 1965 Ford.

Marines

January 2002, Manhattan.

A guy goes into a bar, right? It's a bar in New York. I'm working the 9/11 recovery, and things are pretty quiet. The city is on shutdown by the Department of Homeland Security, but no one feels secure. Lots of talk about bombing Afghanistan. The guy is a Marine, in uniform. I wasn't a Marine but knew several. I'm sitting with a colleague who ignores the guy. People buy the Marine drinks. He gets up and leaves as soon as he can.

Marines! Problematic. It was easier when I saw them as animals; those ground pounders, fast boat gunners, and up-close soldiers. I used to watch them, safe from my ship, doing daring and intimidating stuff as I retreated inside. Later, in the hospital, as I got closer to their pain, I hung out with them, drank with them. I came to see their engagement as comprehensible, at least if you make some wild assumptions about the transience of living and the ephemeral nature of pain.

Still, it was another world, one that was not mine. I felt cowardly and inadequate against that brazen disregard of fear. Hesitant then, conflicted now, I was nevertheless marked, as were most, each according to our own temperament, each to our own hell. Sitting there in the bar at the Hilton, I drank to Marines. Cocktail glasses clinked, voices murmured and then laughed at private jokes. I drank to a lot of Marines, right through the conversation with my work partner, through talk of tactics and what's-gonna-happen next. I sat there somewhere deep and alone, drinking to a bunch of Marines I hardly knew.

I think of Lewis Puller, who killed himself a couple of years ago. The son of "Chesty" Puller, an archetypal Marine, he straddled a similar moral fence to mine, but when your father is the #1 Marine, what do you do? I was feeling Lewis' suicide acutely. Gone. The war is supposed to be over, but so far as many or more vets have now suicided as had died in the field. Lewis was one of those; he'd served in Vietnam, then died because of Vietnam, but his name will never be on the wall, nor will theirs.

Lewis was a writer. He was brilliant, a Pulitzer Prize winner. He checks out, takes an early rotation—commits suicide. It seems he had gone back last year on one of those tours for veterans. I guess he saw what he had done and remembered what had been done to him. Maybe none of it mattered at all. Maybe he just saw that the war was over. I can't help but think that he was trying to make his final amends.

Semper Fi, Lewis!

And I drink to Billy, another lost soul who came to see me in my private practice. Stuff was coming up for him, and he was going to hurt somebody or get arrested if we couldn't stop it. Billy had once been a young marine, ignorant of the ways he could be shaped. The operations had sounded good. So long as it's right, what's a little political assassination? Some terrorism, as long as it's right? In your name he trained for black ops; he was good, infiltrating foreign soil, leading hit teams and mercenary bands to wreak destruction upon hamlets near Hanoi. He was very good. Now he wasn't so young anymore.

It was our tax money and political naïveté that funded his work. He spread terror at our bequest and did some very bad things. Now he's a husband to his third wife, father of four and stepfather to two more. He sleeps little because of his nightmares. He tries to think little because of his flashbacks and thoughts of long ago. He has stopped drinking, for now. Helicopters can set him off for days, and he has come so perilously close to killing others in anger or hurting his own family. His wife fears him, and his children give him wide berth. He is terribly alone.

July 4, 2002, Washington, D.C.

The dark slabs are laced with flowers and tokens. There are fewer this year than last. A few graying Marines still dressed in jungle camouflage haunt the Vietnam Memorial. They are unwilling to let the nation forget, choosing instead to serve themselves up as living testimony to something important. The machine sent them, and the machine sends more, and these Marines bear quiet witness to having been sent. The current regime carries out operations against terrorists, and in so doing, carries out the myriad hidden agendas of vested interests paid for with our money and the blood of Marines.

"Professional Veterans" we call those ghosts at the wall, figuring that they are still stuck in the past and unwilling to live. They sell pins and patches of units that are either gone or have gone on to other things. Anachronistic warriors, perhaps, but I wonder. From their position, I'm guessing that it isn't about keeping a war alive, but rather to keep history in the hands of the people. Billy and Lewis, and all the those lies and truths, live only as long as these Marines can tell their story.

> *Remembering liberty from the Yokusuka Naval Hospital with some Marines on the beach a Kamakura. We've dug a foxhole big enough for the ten of us in the wet sand near the water. Someone has found a bamboo pole, and we've raised an ersatz unit flag fashioned from an old towel. Five or six bottles of whiskey; the Japanese give us a wide berth.*

Grand Rounds

The run up to Baghdad had begun, protestors hit the streets, "Love it or Leave" bumper stickers returned, and I took a call from my friend, Sherry. We had worked together on a mission in St. Lucia, and she'd once had me speak to her Social Work students at the University of Iowa. "I've been working at Walter Reed Army Medical Center," she began.

"What are you doing right now?" she asked in hushed tone over the phone.

I told her, "Believe it or not I'm putting up outdoor Christmas lights with my shirt off." It was one of those absurdly surreal early-December days in California when the Santa Ana winds drove temperatures up over ninety degrees. "What are you doing?"

"It's snowing, and I'm standing in front of the Vietnam Memorial. Nobody's here." Sherry had joined the Army in 1968 when her husband Bruce had flown his cargo plane off the runway in Chu Lai, Vietnam, and had never been seen again. Crazed with grief, she had joined the Army as a flight nurse and flew medevac flights in and out of the same base. She'd spent her time off in the fields and villages near the base, trying to find Bruce, whom she was convinced was still out there somewhere. Thinking of how she obsessed on Bruce's loss, I flash back two years ago. It was the night before she had me lecture on trauma at her nursing school:

> *I'm sleeping on Sherry's living room couch. I'm aware of someone moving in the room. Strong lights flood the outside yard, and I make out Sherry as she slips past the couch and silently takes a concealed position behind*

some drapes. "What's up," I whisper. She motions for me to be quiet, and then, seeing no one outside, explains how she has to walk the perimeter several times a night. You can never tell who is coming over the wall.

"Come and deliver Grand Rounds and tell them what to expect." She referred to my trauma work, of course, and the distinction I drew between single incident exposure and prolonged, repeated exposure to traumatic events. Even those exposed indirectly, through other people's experiences could be affected in the same way. Just the sort of thing WRAMC would get a lot of if the war started.

As a Vietnam vet who abandoned the Navy medical corps, and then my ship, and then the war itself, I felt like the last person who should be telling them what to expect in the field, or from the wounded they would receive at Walter Reed for medical treatment. They already knew about the wounds and the treatment options, and I knew they weren't ready to hear about the close and personal. The hauntings of memory, disillusion, desperation, and death. I had no idea how to give them hope.

*   *   *

The projector didn't work with my specially prepared lecture slides. My handouts didn't get reproduced for me, and then suddenly I found myself approaching the lectern at the hospital, looking up at the sixty or so Army officers, medics, chaplains, and nurses who were waiting for me to make sense for them of the unthinkable, the nightmares they were walking into. Four hours of lecture, without notes.

The longer I spoke, the farther I felt from this audience. They were shifting in their seats, and a few got up and left. The very things I thought most important to tell them were perspectives they would reject as rhetoric and consider defeatist logic. It wasn't about whether the assault on Baghdad was necessary or right. It was about how the wounded would act and how that would affect their care and these people, their caregivers.

1967 Operation Sea Dragon: After eight weeks of firing above the DMZ, friend Al's ship returns to home port in Yokosuka, Japan, where it will undergo repairs and refitting. Al pulls liberty on shore that night, but instead of hitting the bars he stops by the transit barracks on the Base, where, by prearrangement, he meets up with a Corpsman who neatly slices Al's wrists convincingly with a razor. Al then wanders out to the duty Master at Arms, presents his wrists with blood coursing, and is escorted by the Shore Patrol to the psychiatric ward at the hospital. After intake by this same Corpsman, is now hopefully on his way home for discharge.

I found myself allowing enlisted man jargon and profanity to slip into my language talking to the Walter Reed audience. One major officer in the Chaplain Corps raised his hand. "Son," he said. "I don't know where you come from, but the use of profanity is inappropriate." Profanity certainly wasn't inappropriate where I had been, and to use anything less would certainly be. If he was going to the Sandbox, I thought, he'd be hearing plenty more. If he was to try to give comfort to someone with a thousand yard stare and then censor his language, he would paint himself a rear echelon bureaucrat who could never understand

*   *   *

I ignore him and go on.

A Chaplain is swung across by bosun's chair from a supply ship during an underway replenishment of supplies and ammunition one Sunday. We'd been on the firing line for nearly 60 days. He had come to conduct a service on the mess deck. After the service was over I had asked him what God thought about free fire zones (areas thought held by insurgents, sometimes populated by civilians, where we were authorized to fire unused ordnance in order to make room for complete comple-

ments of fresh ammunition). He replied "God has a plan for all of us and all things have a purpose in his eyes. Sailor, just who the hell do you think you are to question God?" I looked back in disbelief.

I notice Sherry in the audience. Her brow knit and her jaw set. Beside her is the colleague I work with from the Foundation, looking equally concerned. I know what it is. Just as clear as a flare against a night jungle sky, their concern wasn't for me. I'm imagining they're worried about how they are going to look given my lapses of podium decorum. I doubt I'll be working for the Army nor the Foundation much longer.

The enormous rear end of the C47 raised up until it sealed in the Medevac flight from Tachikawa AFB near the Naval Hospital at Yokosuka Naval Base. Stretchers stacked three high held bed-bound wounded around the perimeter of the cavernous Military Air Transport cargo plane, while thirty or so ambulatory patients sat facing backward watching the flight nurses labor to keep the prone patients alive. The smell of bodies draining for the eighteen hour flight home mix with the moans of soldiers and sailors weaving in and out of consciousness, too drugged to control themselves. At some point an angel in green scrubs holds my hand.

It was becoming clear to me that I'd come to Walter Reed following some sort of misguided notion of mastering a situation I'd felt defeated by before. I knew that was Sherry's intent for herself all along. Serving again was her way to once again comb the jungle for her lost husband. It was also becoming clear to me that her fight wasn't mine.

I was sad to think that Sherry's credentials in the Army might be tarnished by her having brought me in. Guilt by association is the military way, and I would be branded a radical. I was sad to think that the Foundation would think twice about contracting with me again. Mostly, I was sad to think of some poor kid, perhaps missing a limb or two, perhaps part of his face, trying to talk to that Chaplain in the day room. As if to confirm my fears, the red faced major officer of the Chaplains Corps stands up and stiffly walks out of the auditorium, rigid and unbending. His aide follows close behind. The Army was still the Army.

I so wanted to stop the major and tell him the story told to me by my wife, a former nurse. It seems a doctor, anxious to keep to his schedule, was stopped by the nurse on his way off a ward.

"Just one more set of signatures, Sir, if you don't mind," she said, thrusting a set of forms in front of him."

Pulling his pen out of his shirt pocket, he tried to do so.

"Sir," the nurse cried, pointing at the writing instrument. "That's a rectal thermometer you're trying to sign with."

The doctor looked again. "Hell," he exclaimed. "Some asshole has my pen."

*　　*　　*

Even in 1967 the 1943 Ford Coupe looked like a classic as it pulled onto the the shoulder of the old 395, the two lane highway that connects San Diego to Hesperia. The sailor tossed his sea bag into the back seat. His dress blues dusty and sweaty on the hot June day, the day he was finally discharged from the US Navy. He stopped to knock off some of the dirt before climbing in front. "Thanks, man. I was getting worried no one would stop."

"Glad to. I know not everyone will pick up a serviceman."

"Yeah, well," the sailor smiled. "I'm not sure I would either."

I'd caught a red-eye back from Washington, returning home again. The whole scene back at Walter Reed after the Grand Round lecture—the awkward comments, strained expressions, the clipped remarks—had underlined the unspoken understanding. Sherry was deploying again, in her mind, at least, to search again for Bruce in a new battle. We weren't on the same side.

The early morning sun flared back hot from windows on the 1950's office buildings in south Los Angeles as I drove east on the I-10. I was too early for one of the great hole-in-the-wall fish grill diners on South Central Avenue below the old brewery. At 7 a.m. traffic was moving at a crawl, periodically backed up for no apparent reason. Some of the factory and warehouse buildings in the garment district sported new pastel paint jobs, and billboards beckoned. I watched, bemused and detached, as the vast geometric web of cables and lines, grids and shadows shifted while I rolled slowly through the city, my car radio droning on about the morning opening air attacks on Baghdad.

Then I realized what my eyes had been fixed on as angles and lines developed into familiar shapes. There, just north of the freeway, stretching from the 6th to the 10th floor and twice that distance wide on the East side of a windowless warehouse leered a fresh mural of Picasso's *Guernica*, in the sun. Iconic blacks, whites and grays portrayed the clashing of horses, people, and all the horror that 20th century warfare could rain on an 18th century country village. Some group of war protestors had painted this replica in a clear statement of guerrilla resistance.

I couldn't block the memories of the surreal, muted neon orange of jungle cook fires smouldering against the dark green and black, shadowed jungle background. I could still smell the mix of woodsmoke with burning garbage and sweat smoked clothing.

Supervisory Verbatim #9

Flashbacks

Supervision on a cloudy day, the desk lamps warm against the window. I liked Dr. Williams as a clinical supervisor; experienced, smart, irreverent. We sat in his office, drank hot tea, started with the usual small talk, then got to it. "Hmmm, your face is a bit drawn," he began. "On a mission today?"

"I do have something, yes."

"Did you just get back from something big?"

"Yes and no. I'm back from under my house."

"Oh? This could be good," Williams smiled. "I'm all ears." He settled back in his chair. A former truck driver, feet firmly on the ground, Williams went through a long period in his life when, dissatisfied by the nature of his work, he studied theology. He became a priest, a sky pilot, navigating the firmament. Eventually he tired of symbolic fights, too, and wanted to cut to the human chase. He became a therapist so he could grapple directly with angels and demons.

"So I'm chasing a water leak," I begin. "I heard some dripping and decided to investigate."

"Crawl space?"

"Yeah. I hate going down there; always afraid of snakes and spiders."

" . . . and 'things that go bump in the night'?" Williams smiled.

"And rodents and bugs. Mostly because it's close in and hard to crawl through."

"I'm guessing this is going somewhere."

I scratched my neck. "So I'm down there and I ran into some spider webs with egg sacs. It freaked me out. I started to flash-back about Vietnam—tunnel rats, the guys who went into the cramped tunnels after Viet Cong you know, with a .45, knife, and flashlight—about the spiders and snakes and about people trying to kill each other at such close quarters. Do you know they ambushed us when we were between levels, suddenly bay-onetting upward in the darkness?"

Williams winced. "I didn't know you were a tunnel rat."

"That's the problem. Yeah, I'm a veteran, I was there—close in artillery from a gunboat. Half of our boats got hit from shore. But I was never a ground pounder, and I wasn't a tunnel rat. Ever. But there I was last week, under my house, having flashbacks. And some of those flashbacks were the tunnels."

Williams raised an eyebrow, "You telling me you're having some kind of psychic thing going on?"

"Not at all. I'm telling you that I'm having some sort of imaginary flashbacks. Complete with sights, sounds, and tac-tiles. All the creepy crawlies thrown in."

"What are you feeling when these come on?"

"Like I'm really there, right then. Like I say, I can smell the earth and my sweat. I actually hear the other guy in the dark-ness. I know his family is probably a little farther down the tunnel and I can smell the latrine down there, too. I'm sweat-ing and sticky and smell the funk on my clothing."

"What are you feeling, emotionally?"

"Tense, scared. And then the ship is pitching and the big guns are firing. A North Vietnamese PT boat is charging us and I'm struggling to close a deck hatch before it fires and a guy falls over the side."

Dr. Williams sits up. "Wait a minute, I'm lost here."

"See, that's it. My flashbacks are mixing up real memories with imaginary ones based on stories I've heard. I lived some of it but not all. What's real about all of it is the fear. I feel what I felt then—fear, panic, and sadness. I weep. I can't breathe.

Sometimes it's about things we really did, sometimes it's the same feelings about what happened to other people—like tunnel rats, or the Viets we drove into the tunnels to get away from our shelling, like Vinh Moc."

"Sort that out for me."

"So I was in the blue water Navy, not river patrol, not stationed on land. We did interdiction with coastal vessels—board and search for weapon shipments. But we were also sent on close-in firing in support of infantry operations, both below and above the DMZ. Half our squadron of 12 destroyers were hit by shore firing and missiles. That was part of my flashbacks and dreams—the real things that happened. The other part, about the tunnel rats, was imaginary. I heard a lot about it, and about river patrols, from the scuttlebutt at the time, but also my patients later. But I wasn't there."

"So it's natural you'd have flashbacks, and natural you'd include those of others."

"But I shouldn't do that. I didn't earn the right. Maybe I'm just over-dramatizing, overcompensating."

"Hmm," opined Williams. "Earn the right to a flashback?"

"Yeah, earn it. So if the work is so bad for me, then why am I so easily drawn into trauma drama, why the attraction to big incidents?"

"You know I don't go for a lot of blame gaming about early childhood stuff," Williams cautioned. "It usually doesn't buy us anything. But you've told me about your father being feminized by his parents, and him being violent with you. And sending you off to sheep ranches and cattle ranches to work when you were still in middle school."

"But what does that have to do with 'Nam?"

He smiled. "Just about everything, at least for you. Same with the fires, and now the critical incidents."

"Because I have something to prove?"

"Sure. You told me about the Coyote Fire, about how you got lost in the fight, about being really seen and appreciated for the first time by your Captain. Must have been a revelation to a young man trying to overcome feelings of being inadequate. Remember that book that came out a few years ago, Norman Maclean, *Young Men and Fire*? It's almost a cultural cliché. Could have been titled *Young Men and War*. Or *Young Men and Big Critical Incident Consultation*. Young anybody, but you in particular."

"That one I'll grant you. I don't like it but there it is, just like I don't like the part about being afraid of being an imposter. The flashbacks, though. They don't feel right."

"I disagree. What I think is going on with these flashbacks is pretty normal, if we assume you're normal. You're an empath—you feel what others tell you, you sense what they can't put into words. It makes you a natural therapist because you listen well and you care. But it gets you in trouble. Their stories become part of your experience. Their pain becomes yours and their symptoms become yours, too. Everybody does that to a certain extent, and therapists even more. You, my friend, do it more than most."

Dr. Williams, Th.D. seemed to be warming up. "You walk onto the field of battle with only half a shield. You're more vulnerable than a lot of other therapists to your clients' stories. You're hypnotized by the stories you hear when you consult on those big incidents you seem to be so drawn to, because they are strong stories and you are usually tired and stretched thin. Your problem isn't being inadequate or fragile. Your problem is that you're strong. Your greatest strength is your Achilles heel." He stood up, walked over and looked out the windows at the gathering clouds. "You've got a choice here. Keep up this work and you're likely to get hurt worse than you can repair. You can keep running into the flames because you're good at it and it's good for those who need your help, and it certainly feeds your ego. Or, you can decide you've done enough. You can save yourself."

Revival Sunday

The path leads through the trees, down toward the river. Clouds intermittently block the moon, and he pauses long enough to see again and then moves ahead, cautiously, wishing not to be seen. The muffled sound of water echoes louder. The vegetation grows high on either side of the riverbanks, forming tall sides that reach upward. He crouches in the shadows. Something passes silently, and another cloud comes over the moon. He waits.

The arc light burns overhead, floating back to earth, as things move into slow motion. People run into view, disappearing quickly—an explosion. Then the firing starts.

He wakes abruptly, sweating again.

*　　*　　*

"Oh, Lordy. . . !" My heart sank. The sign in the parking lot read: "Blood of The Lamb Community Church" and in smaller letters, hand-carved into the wood, "Spreading God's Love. " The sun burned through the haze, and I could smell the pine and oak trees in the early morning air. The Pacific Northwest drought I'd heard about was certainly real. Cars nosed into the parking lot as the odd assortment of middle-aged men and occasional families headed for the front door. A church! Jesus Christ, a bunch of holy fucking rollers.

I hesitated. A bearded vet in faded camo jacket walked by, grinning. Longish brown hair, a little matted, fell nearly to his shoulders, and various buttons, peace signs and otherwise, decorated his collars. He looked like he belonged in a place like this. "Come on in, bro. You got this far, man; don't freeze up now!" he called out. His faded vet eyes winked knowingly, but he didn't slow down.

When I'd read the flyer announcing the Vietnam Veteran's Conference two months ago, I had something a little larger in mind, more impersonal, not religious. I'd put in a lifetime as a card-carrying agnostic and had no business here. But I'd scraped together the money and bought a non-refundable ticket. Now there was no hotel shuttle service, no public transport to get me out of here.

Lighting a cigarette, playing for time. My being here had been a long way coming. For fifteen years, I hadn't even classified myself as a vet. I hadn't seen all that much action. Then it had begun coming back in fragments. Nothing big, just bits of imagery. Bites of sound. Dreams. Then I started paying more attention to news reports about other vets. Grinding out my cigarette with resignation, I went on in. I'd come this far. I could always cut out if it got too shitty.

*   *   *

Almost as if it were from a scene out of my Congregational childhood, the folks inside bustled about mixing the smells of coffee with lemon furniture polish and candles, setting up tables and laying down literature. Registration was simple enough, guided through by a middle-aged mid-western looking woman smiling from her loose-fitting cotton dress. "Why, you came a long ways to be here today!" she smiled brightly, her voice loud enough to alert the others. I nodded, signed in, then moved past the entrance.

Unit patches, medals, pictures, and flags graced the tops of tables. It wasn't too dissimilar from the come-on "Welcome U. S. War Hero" signs hung in front of the bars and whorehouses along the streets that led from the base in Subic Bay.

Subic Bay was getting into full swing in 1967 and so was Magsaysay Boulevard. Steamy, drunken nights. A motorcycle roared out the door of a bar, spinning in circles in the street after its driver had been punched right off its seat by an offended onlooker. A bar girl pulled down her white short-shorts to pee in the sawdust on the floor in the dark. I could remember finding myself in a commandeered jeepney full of sailors and marines racing down the main street without its usual driver. I think there was a gun.

Someone behind me tipped over a bulletin board with a muffled crash. I checked my startle reflex in time to notice how many others had frozen for a moment and then resumed what they were doing.

In Yokosuka, a disheveled marine in the psychiatric ward stands in a defensive posture, holding off the other circling patients with a razor blade. Nobody says anything, but everyone maneuvers, weighing their chances of taking him down. Too many drugs, though. No one trusts their reflexes. Finally, the big hayseed corpsman from Nebraska—the one who talked to me for an hour before the windows got punched out—brings the razor-armed marine down with a mattress, so no one is hurt.

The . 50 Caliber machine gun hammers away sounding more distant as I find myself back in the conference.

Still, it seemed more like a church than a conference.

"Good Morning," the conference organizer began. People started moving toward their seats, and I sat down. "Let's open with a prayer . . . " I sighed and wondered if it would be too obvious if I got up now to get a donut and coffee. The organizer got louder, "The Peace of the Lord be with you!"

"And also with you," the congregation answered in unison. I went for coffee.

*   *   *

The program indicated that the day would be spent with speakers and then culminate in an evening worship service. I supposed that was better than face to face with the other vets.

Tomorrow would be a Sunday Morning church service led by the host congregation. Fine then. I'd hear the speakers, leave before it got too intense, and then pass on tomorrow's celebration. Maybe I'd sleep in. The prayer seemed to be wrapping up, so I went back to my seat in the back pew.

"I'm Jack Howard, and I want to welcome you all to the third annual Veteran's Conference. Our first speaker is Bill Cundiff. Bill is uniquely-qualified to share his experiences with us. In 1968, while leading his company on patrol in the Central Highlands, Bill took a machine gun bullet through his spine. Coming home a quadriplegic did not mean the end of his life. He went on to become a minister and the Executive Director of the *Vets in Christ Outreach Ministries*, and I'm sure most of you have heard of Bill or read his book. Let's give a big welcome to Bill Cundiff!"

I could feel the familiar tension that gnawed at my stomach when someone talks about in-country action. I didn't belong here. The applause while Bill maneuvered his motorized wheelchair into position behind the special microphone was genuine, if a little drawn out. After some awkward adjustments and some warm-up comments, Bill began telling his story of being hit, how his life had fallen into despair and self-pity, and how he'd then let Christ back into his life. Bill went on to pursue his theme, "Strong at the Broken Places. "

They served more coffee at the break. Other vets introduced themselves and started conversations. I went back to the sales tables, thinking about broken places. Bill had certainly earned the right to be as clichéd he wanted to be. Bill hadn't quit. I wondered which was worse—sins of commission or sins of omission?

I checked out the war paraphernalia once more, again feeling more than somewhat out of place with these men. The others in the room had earned the right to be here. I'd been so against the war, yet here I am. And why? Am I trying to bask in their reflected glory? I'm standing here feeling almost sentimental for something I hadn't really experienced. I was at the periphery, an unwilling participant, a voyeur.

"How you doing?" The voice startled me, and I looked up. And then down, at the wheelchair. Before me was an intense set of eyes in a large head in a larger body without legs and only one arm. Somehow the chair's occupant pushed himself about with his remaining good arm despite the asymmetry and contrary biodynamics. He smiled broadly. From his buzz-cut and attitude, I figured him for a Marine. "Name's Bud Jensen. Who were you with?"

Navy; a can on Yankee Station. I tightened, half expecting Bud to say, "*Yankee Station wasn't shit!*" Instead: "Sure, I know you guys! You saved my ass a couple of times. "

Oh man. I ought to straighten the guy out. I imagine a smart-assed something like, "*I think you have me confused with someone who gave a shit at the time. *"

What I did say was, "I'm not sure why I came here. "

Bud looked at me steadily. "Well, hang around awhile. Maybe you'll find out. "

*　　*　　*

At lunch, there was no place to eat, so one of the vet families invited me to join them, and we drove into town. The restaurant was right out of Iowa, and so was the family. Everyone else had fried chicken, mashed potatoes and gravy, while I pushed around a salad and felt much too California. They all took turns asking questions—even the two young girls, who seemed taken with this exotic stranger. One asks, "What did you do in the war?" Nobody said anything and everyone studiously chewed their fried chicken.

"I was on a boat," I replied.

"Did you kill anyone?" she persisted. "Daddy did."

Everyone suddenly wanted the peas passed or needed some bread and butter. Isn't the gravy great? I mumbled something, seeing vaporous souls rising out of the shoreline jungle.

"Not directly, exactly," I finally managed. One of the wives looked sympathetic, but no one really knew what to say after that. The gulf got wider. I could hear the artillery in the distance. The arc light shells flooded the midnight shoreline of the jungle with silver light and black shadows. The boat rocked as we drifted, waiting.

*   *   *

The afternoon speakers were a couple. Chris and Dina Toovay. They spoke of the difficulties of being in a relationship with a vet. They were upbeat, but it was a difficult subject and easy to oversimplify. I thought of my house and the patterns of fighting and withdrawal between my wife and myself. How it could be a sanctuary, but how it usually turned out to be a minefield. I remembered how many times I'd wakened out of a dream about an attack or a fire, about rolling out of my bunk, and pitched headfirst into the closet next to the bed. I'd end up slamming my head against the wall and wrestling with yelling sailors under a pile of clothes, still trying to find my boots in time as my first wife was screaming at me to wake up. Or how I woke up more than once on top of her with my hands around her throat. No wonder she'd left my sorry ass.

But mostly, I remembered not really being there. At the most important moments, I'd fade, and find myself hearing distant artillery and rumors of eternity.

Then something unforgettable took us all by surprise. Chris was talking about how hard it is to keep lives balanced. To illustrate, he asked everyone in the room to stand up and balance on one foot. There we all were, all standing up, feeling a little foolish, but grateful to be able to move around after sitting so long. We teetered about, losing our balance and bumping into each other, some lurching forward, or landing on their seats. There was some laughter and murmuring as we grappled with the problem of keeping balance in our lives. Suddenly, it got quiet, and I noticed both Chris and Dina standing at the podium, slack-jawed, staring at something in the back of the room. We all turned to see what it was that had stopped them in their tracks.

There, in the back of the room, quietly balanced on one of his stubs, was Bud Jensen. His eyes burned with determination and triumph as he balanced atop his wheelchair seat. His other stump and the foot-long remainder of his right arm were held out rigidly as counter-weights, and his one good limb was raised in a fist toward the sky. Bud did not waver. We were silent.

*　　*　　*

I decided to go to the evening service after all. I think of it as an anthropologist might, maybe, a chance to study the native peoples in their environment. After all, no one I know would see me here, and I was a bit curious. Besides, the TV reception in the room is lousy, and I was antsy and couldn't bear the idea of just sitting there.

I slide into the last pew a few minutes late, and the service has already begun. There are a few flowered dresses, a few families, but this is mostly for vets. They're all calling out "Welcome home!" And it's worse than I expected. It has everything you'd expect in the hills of Tennessee except rattlesnakes. The imported preacher is on fire, the vets are yelling back "Amen," and "Tell it, Brother!" as if it was a Bob Hope USO show. They sing "Rugged Cross" and "Bringing in the Sheaves." They hold their hands up to the light. Then they sing "Amazing Grace," and I feel the mood shift in the group. A few begin to cry. "Amazing Grace" is one of those songs that does mean something to me, and I hear my own voice mix with the others. I choke up on some of the words. The preacher now tones it down, telling about how we carry the burden of sin with us, and how, if we are going to be right with ourselves, we have to be prepared to lay that burden down.

I see where this is going. I came in as an observer, committed to going along with it out of professional interest. I'm certainly no more than a nominal Christian, maybe more Buddhist, if anything. I figure this probably won't do any harm as long as people don't take it too seriously. But there's no way in hell I'm going to walk down there, in front of God (maybe) and everybody, and go through those motions.

The distance I saw widening at lunch feels as deep as the Gulf of Tonkin. But there's something not right, off center. Maybe it's just me. I'm still not sure I did the right thing back then.

*   *   *

"Hey, are you O. K. ?" the voice repeats. I realize that I am standing alone with tears running down my face, while others are walking up to the cross and kneeling before it. Three men are in front of me. I recognize them as one fighter pilot and the others as two infantry grunts, men I'd heard share stories of extreme fighting and emotion. One was Bud Jensen. "Maybe it's time to lay it down."

Another man persists "What do you need to tell us?"

I can't talk. Tears still come, and words refused to. My throat feels like it's holding a tennis ball. I suddenly get it. Since I wouldn't go down to the cross, the cross had come to me. And it wasn't about believing. It was about them being with me right then and whether I would step across to them.

The words finally start. They find their way through the blockade and begin to flow unevenly. Some of it is intelligible, some isn't. Sentential structure gives way to intensity, and yet they listen to me try and get it out. Somehow, someway, I get it across that I had committed the unutterable sin—I'd gone home and left them behind.

"That war was immoral, wrong," I say.

"Yes, it was." they reply.

"But I left friends there, you there," I moan. "I saw what happened to you guys that stayed. I was on a medevac flight. Guys bleeding out. I saw. "

"Yeah. "

"And . . . " I faltered, breathing heavily.

"And?"

"And I ran away because I was afraid." I go weak at the knees, and they hold me.

"You know what?" they answer, "It just doesn't matter."

"And I don't even believe this Sweet Jesus shit," I blurt. I stand silent, still shaking.

"What do you need?" Bud asks.

"I . . ." whispering, weeping. "I need you guys to forgive me."

"Ha! You're forgiven!" cries Bud with a huge grin, spreading his one arm and laughing delightedly, as if it were a great cosmic joke. "You're forgiven! There! It's just that easy."

These men catch me and hold me while I convulse. They absorb my hurt, my isolation, and I feel their presence.

"I was afraid and I left you," I choke. I let myself be held.

"It's done," repeated Bud. "It's done."

*   *   *

The path leads through the trees down toward the river. Clouds intermittently block the moon, and I pause long enough to see again, and then move ahead, cautiously, wishing not to be seen. The water echoes louder. When he breaks through the trees to the banks of the river, the moonlight reflects off the water and reveals a sandbar that leads to a large rock. In the quiet, I may hear distant singing. The river gleams. Finally, convinced I am alone, I proceed to the sandbar, where I take off my clothes. The chill of the water causes me to shudder. It is cold but feels clean. I wash myself there in the moonlight, my head aching. Afterward I climb upon the rock, taking a Tai-Chi position. My hands caress the tops of the trees and hold the moon, and the cold disappears.

PART III

DARK HOURS AND
BETTER ANGELS

When I was young I didn't understand the evil around me. My family had its share of harmless and not-so-harmless oddities, and the community held its secrets and inequities. A little older, studying philosophy, I explained evil away as absence of good, misdirection, or mistake. God may have had something to do with all three. Much later, following Vietnam, it was clear to me that all of us are capable of evil, if conditions drive us to it. But with this trauma and consulting work came a set of incidents that pushed beyond reason or excuse. They uncovered elements of the world I didn't want to see or know about, dark spirits in close quarters that still shape my days and haunt my nights.

The *Apocalypse Now* character, General Corman, put it well: "There's a conflict in every human heart between the rational and irrational, between good and evil. And good does not always triumph." Murderers, serial killers, rapists, and sociopaths lay the foundation of these new events, and dealing with their aftermath provided me income and prestige. It also sometimes made me want to shower and use mental floss. I desperately wanted the world to work, to be a better place, but was confronted with incidents that provided ample evidence otherwise.

Yet at the same time, in some of the darker hours, I was occasionally surprised to meet people of a very different ilk. These were the souls to whom our sixteenth president Abraham Lincoln had referred in his first inaugural address on March 4, 1861, as the better angels of our nature. I came to notice them, particularly in Los Angeles and New York. They helped me to understand that I had never worked alone.

Supervisory Verbatim #10

Of Darkness and Light

"These incidents," began Dr. Williams, "they get pretty gruesome, don't they?"

"Amen to that," I said.

"So how do you do it? How do you go off to some far-off place, or worse, maybe, somewhere closer to home, to walk on scene as if everything is fine, as if you're perfectly OK doing that sort of thing?"

"Sometimes it is OK," I said. "Sometimes I am perfectly fine. It's exciting to be there."

"But how about those times when it isn't, and you aren't OK. What's it like then? How do you cope with that?" Dr. Williams was giving me the "clinical eye" again.

"I'm expected to project an attitude of 'I've seen it all and know just what to do.' That's half the magic." I felt myself going on the defensive a little. "And when I'm not OK, when I'm scared of the situation and don't know what to do, I fake it. I guess I manage to selectively dissociate, to take note of my feelings, and then put them in a closet somewhere and get on with it."

"You certainly got good at that in Vietnam. And paid a price for it—you've been disconnected for years. Amnesia. Our work would have gone more quickly if you hadn't been dragging around a pretty big sack of leftovers."

I took a breath and let it out slowly. "It may not be perfect, but I guess I get by."

"But surely you can see what it's doing to you. Tell me about the really nasty calls, the ones which go dark on you, and the other ones that leave you more optimistic, bring you hope. And try and tell me how you feel about them."

Esperanza Fire, 2006

Cabazon, California sits on the summit of the San Gorgonio Pass that separates California's Inland Valley from the Mojave Desert. Cabazon is known for its life-sized cement dinosaur/creationist church, a sea of gigantic wind turbines that could daunt Don Quixote, and its huge golden casino. The 310-room Morongo Casino, Resort and Spa towers over the rest of Cabazon. From the top of the 330 ft., 27-floor casino you can see the I-10 Interstate freeway running between Indio to the east, past the Palm Springs turnoff, and then off to the west past Beaumont toward Los Angeles. And should you have been standing atop that casino at five a.m. on October 26, 2006, you could have also looked south to the tall mountains beyond the I-10 and would not have missed those mountains burning. The Esperanza Fire had started at one that morning to the west near the southern edge of Cabazon and by daylight was already three hundred acres and growing fast.

The fire continued its lightning-fast run up the side of the mountain and by 7:15 a.m., hours before the full heat of the day, had burned to death five US Forest Service firefighters, the entire crew of Engine 57. It then went on to consume over 40 thousand acres, 34 homes, 20 outbuildings, totaling some 9 million dollars of associated damage. The local district that had provided that engine crew was devastated by the loss of its own to a fire already determined to be of human origin.

*   *   *

I got there the next day. "See what you can do," I'd been told. I wondered what I could do with as big a situation as this. The folks at the district office had a pretty clear idea. All firefighting personnel from the same district as the fatalities were pulled off the line and were at their stations. "Do some grief sessions" with each crew, plus additional individual sessions with close friends of the deceased. The idea was for me to proceed station by station. "Take two days," they said. "visit every station." I wondered what they thought that meant. The good news was that it pretty much gave me carte blanche to do what I thought was best. The bad news was neither they, nor I, knew what I was getting into. Would I be able to do a good job, here, I wondered?

*   *   *

Most of the stations complied with the mandated sessions, some individuals chose not to participate while others did so both willingly and openly. All were stunned and saddened by the event, some in shock. As I progressed station by station I became aware that the firefighters' reactions were almost predictable by their age group.

Those in their first several years on the job seemed least affected, although it seemed clear that many of them were working at keeping their feelings under tight control. I presumed they were unsure of how much personal disclosure was acceptable for them, as firefighters, to display. My impression was that some of these younger ones were genuinely rattled—mention of burn-overs and safety concerns had been made in fire school, but it isn't something that feels real. Maybe that is part of the denial necessary to force oneself to run into flames when most are going the other way. For these younger firefighters, this was their first exposure to the cold reality of hot fire.

The group of more seasoned firefighters tended to take it all quite seriously. Most knew members of the Engine 57 crew who had died, and were beginning to come to grips with their loss. Most had been in enough fire to understand its unpredictable nature. Most had families and some of those families had made it quite clear that a career change might be a good idea for everyone. And while some of these folks loved fire and had no intention of leaving, others were on the fence about whether or not they could even envision alternatives they could live with. What else could they do, what other career could be so . . . big? This group of experienced firefighters listened carefully to each other and shared what they could.

*   *   *

There was an older group, however, that had something else on their minds. They asked to see me separately after the younger group had finished. I met them at the hot shot station and we gathered in the crew truck bay on folding chairs. There were eight of them, all over 45 or so, some I guessed to be 50. Some were not in firefighter clothing, but rather in dress uniforms with starched creases. I recognized a few from previous jobs I'd done on the forest.

"As you can see, most of us have been around a while," began one of them, "and don't take this wrong, because we really like these kids and feel bad they have to go through it. We knew the 57 crew." The others nodded and looked down. "Some of us are still in the shots, some on engines, and a few of us migrated to desk jobs, but we all started out together on the shots at about the same time. The same fire season."

I waited.

"Here's the deal. On our first year there was a really big fire on this district in backcountry, and our crew was on it. For most of us it was our first big fire. It had burned way up in the high country and helicopters couldn't get in; we had to climb a long ways to get to where we could put in line. We were young, green, excited, enthusiastic, all right, but we didn't know enough to be afraid."

It was clear everyone in the room was waiting for him to get to it. "Things got out of hand. The fire was squirrelly and blew up. Most of us got out to the safety zone, but a couple didn't.

They got burned. Later we found a couple of bodies, one dead."

"The other?" I asked.

"The other was Bob Plummer. Nice guy and liked by everybody. Bob was burned over most of his body, but was still alive." He paused, then continued. "Most of his clothes were burnt off, most of his hair. Even his genitals. We radioed for medical assistance and they started an ambulance and relief crews to help us, but the estimated arrival was three hours. The terrain was rough and the ambulance would take a couple of hours to get close and then the crews would have to hump it the rest of the way."

"So what did you do?"

"We did the only thing we could do. First aid, give him the water we had. Hold his hand."

People around the circle shifted position.

"We held his hand and talked to him," offered another. "It was all we could do."

"He was awake?"

"Not only was he awake, but he knew his chances were nil. He wasn't in much pain. The fire had burned nerve endings and he said he couldn't feel much. He figured he was dying and wanted to talk so we just took turns holding his hand and talking to him as best we could."

"He'd go in and out of consciousness," said a third. "Dehydration and shock."

"What did you talk about?" I asked.

"Stuff. Mostly told stories. He even joked. And he told us not to worry, that we'd done all we could."

*　　*　　*

I left the hot shot station later in the day, wondering if I'd done all I could. We'd told stories, joked. Told each other not to worry.　　　When we had wrapped it up, the eight had stood and held each other. They included me in that circle.

I drove down the mountain, back toward the bright lights of

Cabazon. I couldn't forget what one of the Hispanic firefighters had told me. "You know," he had said. "The word 'Esperanza' in my language means 'hope.'"

> *The cause of the Esperanza Fire was later determined to be arson. Three years later, in 2009, serial arsonist Raymond Lee Oyler was convicted of first-degree murder for deliberately setting the Esperanza Fire that killed 5 firefighters. Mr. Oyler was sentenced to death and is awaiting capital punishment in San Quentin, California.*

Supervisory Verbatim #11:

Too Much?

It was a late afternoon visit, and while still warm, the California sun was already setting and Dr. Williams' lights were already on. We sat facing one another. "You've just gotten back from a fire near the desert," Williams pronounced in a manner more befitting an accusation. "And before that, a suicide in Northern California."

"Mea culpa," I responded. "Two in a week. Both were problematic." I felt the need to explain, so he wouldn't think me an ambulance chaser.

"I read about the fire, it sounds like they've already arrested a suspect for murder."

"Yes," I nodded. "He was overheard in a gas station bragging about how the burn was following his plan. The canyons above Cabazon provide natural chimneys, and the fire just did what fire does."

"And how about the suicide? People just do what people do?"

*　　*　　*

"It was a teenager," I explained. "The parents were out of town and came home to find his body. He'd used a shotgun in the family home. There had been a rash of suicides among young people in the area."

"Why did you get involved in a domestic so far from home?"

"Forest Service family," I said. "The employee assistance company called. They sub-contract with me to provide much of the crisis work for them. The guy who does most of their crisis work involving that area was already out on a call. We cover one another. Sometimes he comes down here. Besides, the family knew me from the Northern California fires several years ago."

I figured that ought to settle the matter. Not so, and Dr. Williams pushed ahead. "You mean that along the length of the state of California, some 800 miles, more or less, no one else was available? Really?"

The reality was that Forest Service Region 5 had given in to the demands of the employees who had received crisis support service from the two of us for years and didn't want to change.

The two of us would respond to incidents up and down the state, and if we were tied up and couldn't, a couple of other therapists from Missoula and Washington State would get on a plane, just like we'd be flown up there if it was necessary. There was also a third soul from the San Diego area. The three of them, like the two of us, were former Forest Service fire people and were trusted. It was a closed circle.

Over the years, we'd taken some heat from others in the emergency psychotherapy community. They said we weren't up to date in the emerging technology of field intervention. This claim never gained much traction because I was on the faculty of the single largest training organization in the country. Not only that, it didn't take many responses for people new to the field to quickly tire of the rigors of crisis response on fire lines.

The fact was that we were pretty much it.

*   *   *

"So you're telling me that you go voluntarily out on these calls, at a certain cost to you in terms of fatigue, hardship for your family, and exposure to difficult human circumstances. Traumas."

"Yes."

"Sometimes more that you absolutely have to."

"Sometimes."

"Well, if you stopped showing up, they'd have to figure out how to get someone else. Some other way of solving their employees' problems."

"And, eventually, I will, whether it's planned or not."

"But not yet?"

"I've still got it; I did it in Northern California. I did it in Cabazon. I like to think that they're better off than they would have been had I not been there."

Dr. Williams gave it some thought and then asked, "Tell me this, though. What is it going to take for you to take care of yourself, your wife's husband, your kid's father, and your student's teacher?"

EMBERS:
A Play in One Scene
by
Kendall Johnson

CHARACTERS

KENDALL: Narrator, a therapist, specialist in crisis management. Called to the station to debrief the engine crew.

CAPTAIN: Head of the station and engine company being debriefed.

ENGINEER: Driver of the fire engine, second in charge of station, crew.

FIREFIGHTER #1: Assigned to the engine, station.

FIREFIGHTER #2: Assigned to the engine, station.

FIREFIGHTER #3: Assigned to the engine, station.

STAGING

In the station conference room, emergency radio can be heard. Upholstered easy chairs, recliners, and office chairs are pulled into an open semi-circle where the crew, including the captain, is sitting. Safety posters hang on the walls, along with pictures of fires and air drops. Kendall's chair is at the back of the circle, center stage, facing front, and sitting just to the left of an easel with markers and a pad of newsprint. A pile of handouts sits under the easel.

(Lights raise to half-light. Crew, including Captain, sit around the circle waiting, some drinking coffee, some cokes. Spot raises on Kendall, entering from stage left. He stands with hands in pockets, surveying the crew, who are frozen.)

KENDALL *(Speaking to audience):*

Some memories age well. They gain a certain patina, a sense of dignity, even, over time. Rough edges get worn off. *(Looks toward group)* Others are different. They are like scenes caught by a strobe's flash, sticking at the edge of our thoughts, ready to race on stage and cast sway over all that transpires. Thus our perception of this moment is colored by our memory of that. Such is the case here. *(Gestures toward group)* A fire crew that recently endured one of those ugly incidents that sometimes befall emergency teams. As the effluvia of urban decay seek their center in the wildland, they occasionally collide. In this case it was motorcycle versus pickup, and the outcome was obvious and messy.

(Turns again toward audience) My role was simple: debrief the tangle. Encourage them to talk about it, share reactions. I get to teach a bit about the normal reactions of normal people to abnormal situations. Their managers have found that talk about the horrors prevents later distress . . . and lawsuits. The complication? Ghosts. Ghosts and ghoulies of the past that make a minefield of the present. *(Walks over to his chair and sits down, lights brightening to full)*

CAPTAIN:

It was last year, that was the thing. We got our hands

real dirty on the motorcycle two days ago, but it was that accident last year that was hard.

ENGINEER: *(Nodding, looking down)*

Roger that—Shit, that was ugly. *(Heads nod agreement.)*

KENDALL:

What happened last year?

ENGINEER:

Well, we were on a strike team, you know, five engines.

CAPTAIN:

We were convoying up the I-5 past Sacramento.

FF #1:

Yeah, I'll never forget that mother.

ENGINEER *(To FF #2)*:

You were there too, weren't you?

FF #2:

Yeah.

KENDALL *(Also to FF #2)*:

Do you remember anything about it?

 (FF #2 looks away)

OK *(Then turns to Captain)*

Weather?

CAPTAIN:

Well, that's the thing. It was dark, and there was intermittent fog. We'd go through these patches of tule fog. Thick, so we had to slow down quickly.

ENGINEER:

I couldn't see shit. We'd be going sixty, and the stars would be out. Then the next thing you'd know, brake lights would light up, and we'd suddenly be in it.

FF#1:

Then we couldn't see anything but the brake lights of the next engine.

ENGINEER:

Yeah. We was just following the lights.

KENDALL:

So, what happened?

CAPTAIN:

So all of a sudden we all slowed down to a stop. After ten minutes of slow and go it became clear there was some kind of accident ahead.

KENDALL *(Looks around at the rest)*:

How were you all feeling at that point?

FF #3:

Well, we couldn't see anything. We knew something was wrong up ahead.

CAPTAIN:

I just wanted to get the hell out of the fog. A fire engine—even these brush rigs—is big and clumsy enough without limited visibility.

ENGINEER:

Me too. We were going maybe five miles an hour. Maybe three. Then the fog starts getting redder and blinking. I figured we were getting close.

CAPTAIN:

Then the strike team leader's voice comes over the mic. He was in the lead truck. I'll never forget it. He says, "Well, folks, it looks like they won't be needing us here."

FF #3:

That asshole.

FF #2:

Confirm that. He was one cold son of a bitch.

KENDALL:

Why?

CAPTAIN:

He wouldn't stop. And when we went by, we could see it all.

ENGINEER (*Shaking his head, almost to himself*):

I will never, ever forget those feet.

FF #2:

Shit yes! That was it. The feet.

CAPTAIN:

Yeah. See, it was a van. A white van, turned over.

FF #3:

And the roof was facing us, and you could see blood on the roof—smeared.

KENDALL:

How'd it get blood on the roof?

CAPTAIN:

And the feet. There were two pairs of feet—real little feet—sticking out from under the van. All lit up by flashing red and blue lights.

(Group is quiet for a moment)

ENGINEER:

Most of us got kids, man.

FF #2:

You don't have to have kids to know it's just wrong to drive away. You know what it's like on those multi-casualty runs. Traffic control, first aid, calling for resources, protecting the accident scene. No one can do it alone. You always need help. I think he's a burn-out.

KENDALL:

The strike team leader? Maybe he was overwhelmed. That's forgivable.

CAPTAIN:

No offense to you, Doc, but here's the kind of guy he is—two miles down the road, he spots a restaurant and calls out "Chow call!", and then pulls off the road for dinner.

ENGINEER:

We were too jacked up to eat. And pissed. Here we are, five engines with full crews, two miles down the road from law enforcement guy working a multi with dead kids, and our strike team leader has his mouth full of corned beef sandwich.

(*Lights fade to half-tone. Kendall—spotlighted again—is motionless for a moment before he looks up at audience. He stands, walks to the edge of stage, and speaks directly to the audience.*)

KENDALL:

So there it is: Bambi meets Godzilla. The real problem of evil isn't so much how God could allow it, but whether it's intentional or just a flaw. I've got enough of a backlog of my own stuff—things that keep me up at night and humble about blame. Yet that strike team leader is still out there on the road, still in charge of folks like these. Do I whistle-blow and then not get asked back next time? Harry Truman said that if you can't stand the heat, then get out of the kitchen.

I try to stay balanced doing this work. I try to keep things in perspective, but the spin seems to be getting more and more off-center. I'm usually fine during the actual debriefings. The ghosts, the implications—they usually set in afterward. That's when it gets dark.

Fade

Chernobyl

Soon after the fall of the USSR, the US State Department attempted to court post-Soviet breakaway republics by offering a variety of programs to entice them into closer relations. One of these was the sharing of disaster response technologies the US had developed in dealing with large natural and human-caused disasters. This international outreach included inviting foreign disaster-management teams to the United States to visit disaster facilities, on-going Emergency Operation Centers, and training institutes.

In my capacity as a trauma shrink and lecturer, I was invited by a local training provider to join his training team and provide an introduction to Disaster Mental Health Principals and Operations to differing State Department funded groups at the California Specialized Training Institute (CSTI) at the old Camp Roberts military base near San Luis Obispo. CSTI excelled in Emergency Operation Center simulation training. Prospective groups included Georgians, Azerbaijanis, and Armenians, all interpreted into their common language–Russian. One such exercise involved a management team from the Ukraine.

In the session, trainees would stand up, yell at me and each other, and shake their fists; this seemed more like a free-for-all than training. Even my interpreter looked worried. I was concerned that the person who had translated my slides into Russian—despite the fact that they were from a reputable university—had for personal or political reasons sabotaged the entire operation. I stood before a hostile group wondering if my slide that should have read "Signs of Trauma" had, in reality, read

"Death to All Ukraine." Both my translator and I struggled through the two-hour lecture.

Afterward, my course coordinator invited me out for a much-needed beer and debriefing. I was certain I was going to be fired from the program.

"Man," I said, "I've never lost control of a group like that before. Was it as bad as it felt? 'Cause if so, you probably brought me here to give me my walking papers."

"Heavens no," he smiled. "They're the group from hell. Literally. You did as well as any of the rest of our trainers." I stared at him. He ordered another beer. "You did great; it was the group. There are a couple of things I didn't want to tell you before the training because I felt it might make it more difficult."

I sighed.

He leaned in, speaking in a softer voice, "The first was the fact that most of the people in the room had been on-scene during the 1986 Chernobyl Meltdown. They were field people then, and most of them got irradiated. A lot of the folks in that room suffered from radiation poisoning to a greater or lesser extent. Some still suffer from radiation-induced psychosis."

I said nothing. I peeled the label corner from my beer. Their behavior made sense; the way they didn't seem to take what I said uncritically, their emotionality about it, their arguments with each other, and their lack of personal control. They had been lied to before. They were OK with the situation and each other, and they knew just where their limits were.

"Another thing I figured I'd better not mention at the time was the composition of the group," he continued. "You just presented to the top managers of the country. Several cabinet members, members of parliament, and the Vice President of the Ukraine."

I was caught speechless. That would explain the one gentleman who didn't yell, but who, when he spoke, commanded respect. He didn't speak often, and when he did, he would make much of pulling himself to his feet and wait until the clamor around him subsided. No one would interrupt, but the yelling would commence once he was again seated. It was probably a good thing I didn't know who was in my audience.

"There's several other things I can share with you now," the course coordinator said as we sipped our beers and watched the sun setting over the hills behind San Luis Obispo. "One is that those guys are the ones who have their fingers on the big red button."

"What red button?"

He looked at me as one might look at a disobedient pet. "They still have possession of the majority of the former USSR's nuclear stockpile. Most of those missiles are still pointed at us."

"Huh . . ." I had to think about their wild eyes and short tempers. "And . . ?"

"The Vice President has been a problem for security. Turns out he's been sneaking past his own security people and ours at night, walking out to the highway, and hitchhiking into San Luis Obispo. He hits as many bars as he can until he passes out."

"So let me get this straight. The Vice President of the Ukraine, the country with the arguably second largest nuclear arsenal in the world pointed at us, slips out past his security people and goes drinking in American cow town beer bars until he's drunk. What could possibly happen with that scenario? One drunk cowboy who has it in for the Russians could take a swing and precipitate a nuclear exchange. Christ. Anything else?"

"Just one more thing. I got a knock on my door two nights ago, in the middle of the night. It was a group of them. They said to me, 'we hear you have a good constitution. We want a copy in Russian.' I spent the rest of the night on the phone to the state department getting a copy of the constitution translated into Russian and faxed to me."

I learned much later that the first phase of writing the current constitution of the Ukraine was begun in 1990, but was not com-

pleted and adopted until June 28, 1996, following several years of discussion, revision, and voting. The Ukraine constitution now requires a tripartite form of representative government: an executive, legislative, and judicial system of checks and balances.

Dark Horse, Idaho

Children all, we must walk
through this world going forth
becoming all that we see, or hear
or feel and then digest—
mind mapping everything we have been.

"Hello, Dr. Johnson? Sorry to call so late. This is Dexter Meadows, Dark Horse Police Department Chaplain. We're in Idaho. I spoke to you in Phoenix a couple of days ago after your talk at the conference. I believe I gave you my card and mentioned I'd be calling. We have a bit of a situation going up here, and I'd like to run it by you and get your take on it and what we ought to do for the community. It's a delicate situation, and we're afraid that, handled wrong, things could go south pretty fast. This is an unusual situation, Dr. Johnson. We're hoping you can give us some suggestions on how to proceed."

By the time Dexter finishes his story, my hair is on end. The police had just arrested one Randall Smit, a 45 year old Caucasian male on charges including kidnapping and child sexual abuse. In the course of investigation they had uncovered evidence of a deeper-level criminal activity. Mr. Smit was currently being held on the initial charges, but the police were reluctant to file further charges because it would quickly attract explosive media attention.

Dexter outlined what they knew already. Smit had moved to the Dark Horse area following his release from prison in Maine two years ago. He lived with his mother in a modest house just off the main street of Dark Horse, near a neighborhood elementary school. An alley cut through the adjacent block, providing a shortcut to and from school for the local kids. He liked little boys.

II.

Our hearts grow darker
as we walk in deeper/ past
revelations of imperfect worlds
We are no longer light spirits
we, too, have become sin.

The Maine Probation Department had been willing to grant Randall's petition to leave the state following his two rather extensive stints in prison. Perhaps they felt that his record of child abductions and molestations was some sort of aberration, or that the fresh air would do him some good. Perhaps they genuinely believed that he would respond well to the combination of his mother's supervision and the counseling he'd promised to receive.

Dexter pointed out that it's been hard for folks in Dark Horse to accept the idea that Maine would let an obviously dangerous child sex offender loose among them, especially with no warning. Idaho residents tend to be friendly and welcoming. It is a big country, and there can be a lot of miles between one person and the next. Maybe it's that big cold sky that brings out the sociability.

Smit came to live with his mother, near the home of 10-year-old Micah Jones.

"Dr. Johnson, we got a complication, a kind of situation here. We've found evidence suggesting cannibalism. Human bones were found under his house, with writings that make us think he cooked and ate at least some of his victims. We need more time to process the evidence and file the new charges, but that seems to be what happened."

"So you're afraid of community agitation and you're looking for a way to get the relevant information out without setting off panic or vigilante action?" I asked.

"The newspaper—the owner lives in this town—agreed to give us two days to figure out how to release the information in a manner that keeps it from throwing the community into panic. It isn't clear just how many other children beside Micah met their fates at the hands of Randall Smit. The bones they found under his house were the bones of children. The DNA tests run on those bones show that they did not belong to Micah. There is no DNA match between those bones and the tissue samples of the other children in the Dark Horse area who had disappeared. But . . ."

"It gets worse?"

"Turns out Smit joined a church. Not only did he attend, but he really got into it, became some sort of lay leader or something. He organized meetings at his home and invited parishioners in to share meals and fellowship."

I thought for a minute. "You don't mean . . ."

"'Fraid so, Doc," Dexter said.

Dexter went on with more detail. There were detailed journals for "little boy stew," "little boy pot pie," and lunch served *al fresco* "with roast child." Imagine the mix of guilt and victimization the church congregation would feel when they receive the news that the "peculiar tasting meat dish" served up by Smit was so much more than they had expected.

"The folks around here are tough and can take bad news, but this is pretty much over the top. Before this goes public, we need to find a way to get this out to those church people so that they get a chance to deal with it. All it would take would be one underpaid newsroom flunky to drop a dime to CNN for a big cash reward. Those church folks should all find out at once and have a chance to begin working it through before they see it on Channel 3 news. We'd appreciate any suggestions as to how to do that.

"Doc? You still there? Sorry, I thought we lost the connection for a minute."

"Uh, yeah. We're good."

III.

*If the eater's heart is clean, there's no more sin
taken on, if the stain has not fallen on
fertile fields or our pilgrim not be fallen
more dire circumstance, he or she should
be alright and it should all work out.*

I outlined a plan with Dexter that was carried out in the days before I could get there. Planning is always the easiest part. Doing it is harder, but they did their jobs well. In anticipation of the sudden horror that would hit those who'd been a part of the macabre ritual, the church called in those families who'd been to the servings and gave them the news in the presence of lay counselors, family therapists, and child specialists. Those immediately involved were encouraged to talk it out, to ask questions, to ask the professionals about what to expect and how to help their children and start the process of making sense.

As the parishioners were having the news broken to them, the schools had called in their students' families and told the news in a controlled setting so that all would know at once. The local newspaper worked with the police's public information spokesperson and psychologists to present the story in the least shocking manner on the same day. The community was informed before the TV trucks hit town. Textbook operation. Clean. By phone.

I missed the hard part, the face to face.

But I thought about it. Telephoned them. Researched it. Sent more plans. Dreamt about it. Dreamt about it again. And again.

In one of our calls, Dexter asked me a simple question: "What do I do for my people?"

IV.

Now it's true that earth's cleansing

accrues to us with the passing of suns and tides,
in seasons of good winds and rains;
They wash our heart's burdens, granting
absolution's promise for even the sin eaters.

Randall Smit had set a ghastly table there in Dark Horse, inviting others on false pretenses to break bread and share with his host. They were ignorant of his actions, dining on their own children as innocent as Thyestes, Seneca's mythic victim of vengeance who then, in his anguish, perpetrated more vengeance. Revenge plays out through generations all over the world—in Rwanda, Bosnia, Afghanistan, and in Dark Horse, Idaho. We don't know what horrors lay behind Smit's obsessions, and we don't want to care. When the big out-of-town news agencies broke the story, the town would be horrified to discover what they had done. The entire community lost its innocence along with Micah Jones. True evil had come to visit Dark Horse.

And evil had come to visit me. So, like any good shrink, I went to see my shrink, before my scheduled visit. As the people of Dark Horse were doing the meetings, the press releases, the conferences, the hand holding and kleenex passing, I was seeing my therapist.

It was quiet in his office.

"So that's about it," I concluded.

"Holy smokes," he remarked.

"Not much holy about any of it."

"No. So what are you going to do now?" he asked.

"Do? I'm scheduled to go up next week and give the emergency people a debriefing. Run over what they did, how it worked, and what they need to do."

"And?" he said.

"Isn't that enough already?"

"And how to take care of themselves, their families, their organization? Hell, man, the bonds of social contract got broken here. The use of socially prescribed form, friendship, and the church were twisted in pursuit of the guy's perverse personal gratification. It violated the MDRC— the Minimal Daily Required dose of Civilization. The symbols and structures of religion carry this act to another dimension. Off the chart."

I was quiet.

V.

Were we pure of spirit, we would not reflect
the earth's dark blemished face;
nor would we need confessors, therapists,
shaman or the other sin eaters to pick
our stained souls white again.

It wasn't until I arrived in Dark Horse a week later that the community was settling back into some sort of normal—if more vigilant—routine. There were aftershocks, and there would be many more. The schools, the clinics, the pastors, and counselors would spend years digging out from the leftovers of this bad meal. You didn't have to eat from the pot to smell the pie and taste the stew.

It was the police, the emergency and medical people, the school teachers and counselors, the therapists and the clergy who had been touched by the stories again and again, who would carry it home from work. Dexter's last question still haunted me: "What do I do for my people?"

One caveat stands between the transient
and his free, if uncomfortable meal.
When he dies he will be held accountable
for all he has become. Late payments await,
with interest fairly accrued.

Driving back from the airport after getting in from Idaho, I noticed a sign in a health food store window. It read: "You are what you eat."

DARK HORSE EPISTOLARY

Christopher Williams, Th.D.

Clinical Psychologist

December 23, 2000
Kendall Johnson, Ph.D.
Re: Supervisory Follow Up

Dear Dr. Johnson,

For the most part, I've enjoyed working as your clinical supervising therapist over the past several years. I'd be a liar if I said I enjoyed our session this last week. Just hearing it second- and third-hand was hard enough. I'm not sure there is enough mental floss to take care of cases like that.

I'm going to be off at a conference starting Thursday, and then you leave for Dark Horse before I return. I've had a couple of additional thoughts about your case and found a book that has a perspective you might find helpful. I'll jot it down here so you get it before you leave.

As you know I'm trained in theology, not just psychology. This case pretty much straddles that fence. Randall Smit became a priest of darkness up there in Dark Horse, maybe even a god. His was the power of life and death, and he exercised that will to subordinate others to his ends. He set the altar in his kitchen and sacrificed young lambs. When it pleased him, he brought in the community share the toxin in his own special way. The man was more than disturbed. He embodied evil.

You asked me how to be present there, in Dark Horse, listening to the folk's shock and pain and still manage not to get hurt. The short answer? You can't. Lots of therapists get hurt by their clients. Someday I'm going to write a book for shrinks: *How Not To Get Hurt While Sitting In the Chair*. I think it will sell. Don't ask me for supporting data. I'm a lotus-eater. It's an old fashioned case study based on observing other therapists like you.

I'm just now looking at a review of a book that came out last month. *The Sin Eater: Perils of Compassion*. I quote: *"Irish folklore contains much wisdom distilled into story form. One such story is The Sin Eater. According to some traditions when someone dies, its soul will not be released as long as it's burdened with sins. It is tied to the earth like Hamlet's ghost. The Sin Eater, a social outcast, if fed a meal on the corpse's chest, can take on the sins, freeing up the recently deceased for the next world."*

Another excerpt: *"Now it's true that earth's cleansing accrues to us with the passing of suns and tides, seasons of good winds and rains wash our heart's burdens granting Absolution's promise for Sin eaters as well."*

Kendall, I'm guessing you've about decided that I'm coming down with a case of old-timer's disease, but hear me out. I'm not saying you need to see a sin eater. I'm saying that you *are* the sin eater, going around soaking up the evils of the world. The world is a broken place, and you're knee-deep in the breaks. You seek them out!

One last quote from the book for you to think about before you go up to Dark Horse: *"Were we pure of spirit we would not reflect the earth's dark blemished face; nor would we need confessors, therapists, shaman or other sin eaters to pick our stained souls white again."*

With all due respect, I think you're going to need more than a therapist when you get back from Dark Horse. Consider an exorcism.

Sincerely yours,
Christopher Williams, Th.D.

ANGELS IN THERAPY:

A Play in Two Acts

by

Kendall Johnson

CHARACTERS

KENDALL: A therapist, specialist in crisis management
DR WILLIAMS: Kendall's supervising therapist
SARAH: Head of County Post Disaster Outreach Project
ALICE: Middle School Teacher, patient of Kendall. Referred by Outreach Project.
BRAD: A young, aspiring actor, patient of Kendall. Referred by Outreach Project.
DAVIS: A middle-aged black industrial plant manager, patient of Kendall. Referred by Outreach Project.

STAGING

Stage setting is complex, with front center devoted to Dr. Williams' office: two comfortable swivel chairs facing 45 degrees away from each other, toward the audience. Several small tables are arranged in a homey manner, with a plant, lamp, telephone charger, and radio. Dr. Williams' chair is on stage left, client's chair on stage right. Several such workplace settings are set around the stage periphery, including, from stage far right to left:

1. A corner of a classroom (several student desks, a

teacher's desk, assorted posters and announcements on the wall). Tidy but run down.

2. An industrial plant office, with middle management desk & window with a factory scene. Production graphics on wall.

3. An agency office with three identical desks in cubicles separated by partitions. Telephone ringing and extra people in office clothing walk back and forth carrying papers.

4. Kendall's office, more utilitarian than Dr. Williams' office, positioned with a high stool so he can pivot to look directly at each of the other characters when necessary for dialogue.

Behind each work space is a large screen for projecting photographic images.

The stage will be dark upon opening, and only those areas involved in each scene will be spotlit. Sounds, projected images, and half light will be utilized as indicated for each scene.

ACT I

Scene 1

BRAD:

I act. Only in bit parts so far. I'm thirty years old and waiting tables. It's cliché. But, hey, the tips are good, and it leaves my days free to beat the streets. Yeah, I have a house. 1500 square feet of cracked plaster and poured concrete. Like I said, I'm basically a family man. Bills to pay, but at least my kids have a neighborhood. And then there's the other. Hollywood, that's the deal.

KENDALL:

What is it that acting gives you?

BRAD:

I don't know, can't really describe it. It's as if something happens out there. On stage. I'm nervous as hell—right up until I step out into the light. At that very moment everything changes. Something—someone—takes over, and it's magic. Things work, and it's more real than real. And it is. And a lot more important; a lot more important.

KENDALL:

Where's the downside?

BRAD:

(images of West LA & San Fernando are projected in Brad's space)

The business. Hollywood and West LA. It's bitchy. Gossipy. Half the time it bores me and the rest I'm sucked into it. Everybody's self conscious there. They're on stage when they stop to get gas. The business is all there is there. In the industry, the casting directors couldn't care less if you've got to pick up your kid from soccer at 6:00—unless you've got a name. But then if you've got a name, your kid can't play soccer. It's not safe. They'll get snatched.

So there I am in the Valley; being dutiful Dad, missing out on parts. It's got to be like that. You can't raise kids in Hollywood. There, everybody's hustling, everything's fast. Down and dirty. The pretense IS the point. Cut grass, sprinklers, toys on the driveway. Thirty minutes later I'm in Hollywood. San Fernando to Fellini on a freeway.

KENDALL:

I understand you were out of town for a week.

BRAD:

New York. Bit part.

KENDALL:

How did things go?

BRAD:

You mean the job or personally?

KENDALL:

Either.

BRAD:

The incredible thing was being away from home. I got clear on two things. The first was that I really want to be with my family. San Fernando's all right. The second thing, though, is that I really loved being alone in New York.

KENDALL:

It's a pretty exciting place.

BRAD:

There's something about it that LA hasn't got. A sense of place, maybe. Community. Even though it's so huge, it hangs together.

(Lights dim over Brad)

Scene 2

(Lights raise over Alice's classroom. Alice stands to greet Kendall enters)

ALICE:

Thank you for visiting my classroom.

(Slumps into the chair at her desk)

I don't know what's wrong with me anymore.

KENDALL:

Like what?

ALICE:

Oh... I'm tired; I just don't care about stuff *(pauses, sighs a little)*. I used to... care, I mean. I used to prepare my lessons the week before, keep up on corrections, read the literature. Decorate my room. I used to go off to conferences to get new ideas, find inspiration. Now I just go to get a day off. I don't want any new ideas—they mean work.

(spot raises on her room to half light)

Every day I face those kids. I don't know... It's their eyes, I guess. They've all seen too much. *(images of earthquake destruction)*

I am plagued by the earthquake. I can't shake this one off. When I look at the pictures, it just seems like the end.

KENDALL:

I wonder why...

ALICE:

(images of social deterioration; she thinks for a moment)

I suppose it has to do with the whole area. I grew up twenty-five miles east of LA, when the area was going from agriculture to defense and bedroom communities. It was still a small town, then. Then my town, the one I grew up in, went from a middle class bedroom community to an... I don't know what. It got run down. Gangs moved in. There is graffiti everywhere.

KENDALL:

Not good changes.

ALICE:

No, and it gets worse. The whole area is like that. Nobody cares anymore. Nobody belongs. The Earthquake pictures remind me of that. The earthquake didn't do as much harm as the people did. It just did it faster. Everything has turned upside down.

(gets up, moves into class area, it lights up fully, Kendall swivels to face her; images fade)

I see it in my classes. My students come from terrible home situations. But there's something worse that I can't quite put my finger on. There's no sense of history, no permanence. And no values.

(she sighs, slumping into a student's chair)

I look into their eyes, and there's something missing. I got this one kid in class. His name's Dontai. *(pronounced Dante)* Dontai, can you imagine? He's back in school now after a couple of years of being passed back and forth. His mother traded him for a truck.

KENDALL:

(Incredulously) A truck?

ALICE:

Really. It was part of the divorce settlement. Then last week he goes to visit his real dad. Hadn't seen him for years. Dad has a heart attack. Dies while Dontai's trying to give him CPR.

KENDALL:

My God!

ALICE:

It rubs off. When I get too tired, I lose my defense against it. The world starts to look gray. I start seeing things from their perspective and I feel helpless and hopeless.

KENDALL:

And...

ALICE:

... And scared. One of our teachers was attacked on his way to his car last week and beaten with bats. You know what I mean. It's like the sixties are really over.

KENDALL:

How's that?

ALICE:

I had all these romantic ideas about helping children—Teach for America!—but it's not that easy. I never thought I'd become a union organizer, but I'm the building rep for the teacher's union. And everything's a power fight with administration. Everything! They try to take away non-cost benefits like enforcing an extra half hour duty even though we don't have kids on campus at that time. It's like they can't just not fight.

KENDALL:

So if you go the extra mile for the kids, you are giving in to the administration.

ALICE:

I'll tell you what it's like in the classroom. Remember that kid Dontai? Well, when I was talking to Dantai about his father dying in his arms, you know what he said? I'm just sitting there listening to him. He said that after all those years of not having a dad, at least he could kiss him good-bye! The CPR! That was his kiss good-bye! Christ! And he cried ...

FADE

Scene 3

(Light raises to Davis' office in an industrial plant. Davis is standing, looking out the window. Kendall is standing, facing Davis' back)

DAVIS:

I've always been able to take care of my own business. It's just that... that things are getting out of hand. I can't sleep like I should. Like I have nightmares a lot. Can't relax. Something's not right. I'm tired all the time. Wore out.

KENDALL:

What sort of work do you do for the company?

DAVIS:

I'm the plant manager. Tire recapping. I've worked there now for twenty five years. Started with a broom and ended up on top. Proud of it, too. When things are cookin' we turn out a lot of tires and cut a lot of pay-checks. It helps the community. I've got people there I've known for years. Some I started with. Up 'til a few years ago it was like family.

KENDALL:

What happened?

DAVIS:

I don't know, maybe I'm just losin' it. The juice, you

know? Everything's coming undone. I can't seem to get it back. Started during the unrest two years ago.

KENDALL:

I didn't realize that plant was hit.

DAVIS:

No, it didn't affect the plant. We closed down and tripled security. We were OK. My workers were a mess for a couple of months and production slipped, but we got through it. *(pauses, looks away)* Somethin' strange started happening, though. I'm not sure, but I'd be looking out a window or driving down the street, and it was just like I was seeing it all over again.

KENDALL:

The unrest?

DAVIS:

No, man, the riots. I mean '65. Watts. It was different. The times. There was a lot of agitation, change was in the air. Civil rights protests. Voter registration. But it wasn't happenin' in Watts. Things finally blew. I was scared. Things were crazy for days. I got hit. Threw rocks. I almost got shot. For a couple of days, we didn't know if they were going to shoot us all or not.

KENDALL:

You got shot at?

DAVIS:

I came close. Me and a couple of guys was running up this alley, and two cop cars headed us off. It was at night, see, and in that alley it was just headlights, red lights and dark. *(becomes transfixed, staring ahead)* They had us up against a fence and started hassling us. Billy ran, man, and they did him. The cop that shot him was standing right behind me, and I yelled. The muzzle flash lit up the rest of the alley and I'll never forget Billy flying forward and into the dirt. Then something hit me on the back of the head and I went out. *(resumes focus on the present, looks back at Kendall)* I can't remember what it was I was screaming, though, whatever it was I think I need to remember. That dream, though. It keeps comin' back. I'm yelling something to Billy, then the flash. What was I trying to say?

FADE

Scene 4

(Spotlight rises on Agency cubicle. Kendall is sitting on a chair pulled up to Sarah's desk. Others are dimly seen at their cubicles, extras bustle by carrying papers. Telephones ring.)

SARAH:

Thank you so much for coming down. I promise I'll break loose and come to your office next time. I really need to get out of here for a while anyway.

KENDALL:

It's quite alright, but why can't you get out of the office? You know, to get some time for yourself?

SARAH:

We have deadlines waiting in line. I'm glad you offered

to talk here. If I don't get a handle on the stress in this place, I don't know what'll happen.

KENDALL:

So what's going on?

SARAH:

We are trying to transition from immediate services following the earthquake to an extended services grant. We have to get that to be able to provide what we said we'd provide under the immediate service grant.

KENDALL:

Which was?

SARAH:

To provide initial crisis intervention and prepare for the intermediate phase. I'm trying to provide support to my field people and I'm tied to this computer. I have to put out this proposal. The Feds are screaming for it, my boss is screaming for it, and my field people are trying to make do with what they've got. Some of my emergency centers don't have phones, or even Xeroxes. I don't even have time to conduct interviews to hire enough field people. Look at that pile of stuff. Workbooks for kids and handout information sheets for families. They need these and we can't release them!

KENDALL:

The books and papers? They're just sitting here?

SARAH:

I can't release it because release hasn't been approved.

KENDALL:

But you had approval before you ordered it, didn't you?

SARAH:

No, I ordered it with verbal approval because we had verbal approval on the original proposal.

KENDALL:

So it's approved, right? I'm confused.

SARAH:

I know, but the verbal approval was amended.

KENDALL:

So you should have waited for written approval?

SARAH:

No, I couldn't wait for written approval to order it because if I waited, and it was approved, then it would have taken the printer too long to get it delivered.

KENDALL:

Too long? In what sense?

SARAH:

In the sense that the ending date of the grant for immediate services would have elapsed.

KENDALL:

Is that a problem? Surely the money could be carried over...

SARAH:

Oh no! Materials cannot be paid for until delivery, and all money must be dedicated before the date of elapse. Sure I could buy it on the extension grant money, but we haven't got verbal approval for that grant yet. Besides, that grant may not be able to afford materials like that.

KENDALL:

So the materials are sitting here when they should be in use out in the field. Where does it break down?

SARAH:

Somewhere up the line. Bosses keep changing the rules. First, they say we've got Federal money to burn and to spend it fast. Then they say do it right and document it. Then they say we've only got half as much. Then they say to maximize our service recipient numbers. Then they say that we have to 'give impetus for lasting change.' Then they say that we don't fit the Federal project guidelines anymore. Then the hot issue becomes controlling the quality of our contractors, like you. Now they're complaining because we're late. We should have been delivering in the field a month ago! *No matter* how much I want to help, I feel like I'm part of the problem.

FADE

ACT II

(Kendall and Dr. Williams in supervisory session)

DR WILLIAMS:

(Affecting an exaggerated Freudian inflection) Und zo, just who do you tink you are; zomeone who flies above the ground on winks?

KENDALL:

(Looking away) Me?

DR WILLIAMS:

You tink ze pains of everyone else cannot touch you? *(Resuming normal inflection)* You are a lightning rod, a transformer. They process through you. You pick it up.

KENDALL:

(Quiet for a moment) LA is such a crazy place. I'm having my clients write in their journals this week about living here.

(Lights raise to half tone over the four clients, who are busy writing at their desks in their separate work-places. Each speaks when indicated, initially eyes down, reading from their journals.)

BRAD & SARAH:

(In unison)

We are L.A.

Once lotus land of Buicks,

fast breaks and suntans,

of orange grove Disneylands.

We ride inexorable waves of change,

the products of global shift.

DR WILLIAMS:

Crazy? Hmm. I think not; more like too transient. L.A.'s problem is more like a personality disorder.

KENDALL:

As in character disturbance?

DR WILLIAMS:

Sure. Think about it. It's built on shifting sands; fault lines. Flaws in its very structure.

KENDALL:

Like conflicting cultures?

DAVIS:

Human tectonic plates
colliding along LA's fault line matrices
(faults are, after all, relative to position).
We are grinding, crumpling, fraying
fracturing out periodic releases
uneven discharges so intense
that even obdurate, bureaucratic paralysis
can not contain the blast.

DR WILLIAMS:

More than that. Below the diversity, there is a lack of being grounded. No sense of place. Everybody's an immigrant.

KENDALL:

I'm not. Third-generation native. Same town.

DR WILLIAMS:

L.A.'s the only place this side of Anchorage where third-generation means anything. And it doesn't mean a thing here because nobody really gives a rip. We're a pack of get-rich-quick artists. Gypsies. Transients looking for opportunity. LA is a city of opportunists.

(Lights raise variously on each of the other cast members singly or together as indicated:)

ALICE:

We crystallize the world;

macro-change playing out painfully

(add a line of imagery/specificity related to the abstract above)

in our Angel's days and dreams.

KENDALL:

Except for natives.

DR WILLIAMS:

Third generation? So what brought your great-grandfather here?

KENDALL:

He put in one of the first water wells in Pomona Valley.

DR WILLIAMS:

And sold water to the rest of the immigrants. How about your grandfather?

KENDALL:

Sold real estate.

DR WILLIAMS:

Your Father?

KENDALL:

Sold insurance to the people who bought his father's real estate. All right, I get the point.

DAVIS, ALICE, BRAD & SARAH:

(Unison)

We are LA.

Our children float,

our promises are incomplete.

Their futures are uncertain

while we stand hypnotized by

biannual disaster

as our faults strain harder.

DR WILLIAMS:

A city of hustlers.

KENDALL:

All right, I'm game. So what kind of personality disorder?

DR WILLIAMS:

Borderline.

KENDALL:

You're diagnosing LA as suffering from Borderline Personality Disorder? Which border?

DR WILLIAMS:

I'm serious. American Psychiatric Association Diagnostic Manual: eight criteria, only five necessary for diagnosis. I'll read them. *(Picks up a green book, turns to a previously marked page. Quotes:)* "Borderline Personality Disorder: A pervasive pattern of instability of mood, interpersonal relationships and self image... Criteria number one: a pattern of unstable and intense interpersonal relationships characterized by alternating between extremes of over-idealization and devaluation.

KENDALL:

Hmm. Check. We see ourselves as having the perfect climate, freedom of ideas, and healthy lifestyle. Yet it's a self-avowed rat race, we cut each other's throats in a moment, and tolerate any amount of poverty and crime in order to give ourselves a chance. Yeah, that's pretty unstable and extreme.

DAVIS, ALICE, BRAD & SARAH:

(Unison, but gradually standing, looking directly at the audience)

We are LA

The dark side of the juggernaut 40's,

50's civil war, the 60's and progressive

post-enlightenment decades of

drift and self-absorption

culminating in 90's now—

the age of Karma and collections

—our wages of sin.

DR WILLIAMS:

Criteria 2: Impulsiveness in at least two areas that are potentially self damaging, e.g., spending, sex, substance use, shoplifting, reckless driving, binge eating.

KENDALL:

(Laughs) OK

DR WILLIAMS:

Criteria 3: marked shifts in mood from depression to irritability, or anxiety.

KENDALL:

Keep going.

DR WILLIAMS:

4: inappropriate, intense anger or lack of control of anger, e.g., frequent displays of temper, constant anger, recurrent physical fights.

KENDALL:

Hey, not fair! Been to New York lately?

DAVIS, ALICE, BRAD & SARAH:

(Unison, more softly, sitting and looking at their books)
We are LA—
One golden thread uniting us:
the full pot naively attempting to meld
the whole lot of suffering
opportunist incommensurables.
We are, all of us, gold rush kings
and queens of the night
who have run out of credit
...and we, having soiled the nest,

seek to fly home.

DR WILLIAMS:

Criteria 5: recurrent suicidal threats, gestures, or behavior, or self-mutilating behavior.

KENDALL:

East LA, South Central, Venice, Sunset Strip. All except Beverly Hills.

DR WILLIAMS:

And they're not choking on their own effluence? Or burying the rest? Look, the Westside/Eastside cultural and economic split isn't as easy to discern anymore. I guess the good news is that it isn't as Schizoid as it used to be. The dissociation is more self directed. *(Resumes reading)* Criteria 6: marked or persistent identity disturbance manifested uncertainty about self image, sexual orientation, long term goals, preferred values.

KENDALL:

Ouch. That sounds like the agency. Hell, it sounds like most of us to a greater or lesser degree. Even my dog; he's trying to decide whether he's straight or gay. Suppose we should move out of LA?

DR WILLIAMS:

Wait, there's one more:... number 7: frantic efforts to avoid real or imagined abandonment.

KENDALL:

That one's kind of interesting. We seem to seek private space and time, yet we bring along our TVs and cellphones. If we get stuck with a free evening, we flip channels.

DR WILLIAMS:

According to the book, only five of the eight are necessary for diagnosis.

KENDALL:

So you're concluding that the entire region suffers from a massive case of Borderline Personality Disorder. That's funny. *(Pauses)* That's scary. That means every one of us has it? What about the healthy ones? What about the "normal" depressives, anxiety cases, or addicts? How about the relationship problems or mid-life crises? What about my clients? Most of them aren't Borderline disorders.

DR WILLIAMS:

No, they're not. But they are the products of their environment. They are like children of a dysfunctional family. The borderline condition of their social family exacerbates their individual symptoms. LA seeps up through our feet. It grabs us by our soul.

(Lights over KENDALL and Williams fade to half tone; raise to full over:)

BRAD, DAVIS, ALICE, AND SARAH:

(Unison, standing, full voice, looking directly at audience)
We are LA,

haunted by visions of endless change

without transformation.

We tremble on the edge of future,

praying for relief,

questioning hope,

unwilling to release.

We are LA.

We are the new, fractured world

we strain against ourselves.

FADE

O'Brien's Boat

On the morning of September 11, at 5:45 a.m., I had just got my coffee made, and was sitting down to read the morning paper, enjoying the moment of calm before waking up the rest of the house. I teach at-risk kids. I'm a trauma therapist and a crisis consultant. You'd think getting my kids off to school wouldn't be the hardest part of my day, but there you go. So there I was, six weeks ago, digging the quiet of the morning. I heard something.

Not loud. Not even a drip, really—more like a tiny trickle far away. Until I got down close to the base of the toilet and listened very carefully. Damn! Drip for sure, and not only that, it sounded like it was falling into something bigger. All I wanted is a few more moments of calm, and then this happened. And then the phone rings, and well, after that, I forgot all about the drip. "Are you watching the news?" my school principal asked. "Meet me down here as soon as you can." I turned the TV on.

> *How slowly the building slid away. How gracefully the dust column fell in upon itself. The familiar blanket of dissociation covered me as if it were so much ash. I marveled at my mind's struggle to sort through impossible images while at the same time coiling to act. "What now must I do?" a voice calls from far away. No single event could be this enormous. The voice was closer now, "What now must I do?" I could hear it counting: one, two, three, take a breath, four, five, the building fell once more, six, I started up off my knees, reaching for the "off" switch, seven, lurching toward the phone, eight, the number came to me, nine, I am raising the receiver to my ear, ten.*

I bring the phone to my face, shaking off the trance. "Hey buddy," I asked my colleague who runs the crisis team I train, "are you watching the news?"

II.

The rest of the day turned out predictably unpredictable. I was handed control of the school because the principal was called to the district office to decide what to do. At least a substitute was provided so I could make calls to my Long Beach crisis team and the New York Chancellor's office—at least until the communication center in the second tower collapsed—and keep the TVs turned off in the school.

I watched George W. Bush on TV that night. This time he had his "determined leader" mask on and Congress was united in support. I guessed that George W. had finally found his niche. The front row was a solid phalanx of Generals and Admirals. Even the Supreme Court justices (at least those who could stay up that late) stood when he sounded the call to arms. A long, protracted war, he promised. Get at the root of the problem. Victory, he promised.

III.

Three weeks later and my work is slowing; I still haven't been invited to New York. What now must I do? Will the "Love it or Leave it!" bumper stickers of the Vietnam days come back? Will the opposition party be again branded as "effete, intellectual snobs?" Maybe Manzinar will re-open. I wonder how many senators will still be sharing the cheer when the body bags started coming home, and their constituents have taken the flags off their cars.

Of course, George W said nothing about a draft yet, but I have to think of the chair loads of cannon fodder to whom I teach writing and art at school. Just yesterday I received word that yet another had been killed in an industrial accident. I remember Marc, and how sweet, guileless, and just plain dumb he was. Of course he'd been in the wrong place at the wrong time—the sort of thing that accounts for most wartime casualties. I'm thinking of Tony Franco back in 'Nam. He'd bumbled the loading of a 5" 50 artillery shell and blew his thumb out in the heavens somewhere over the Demilitarized Zone. How many of my students will get sucked up in this "operation" out of that predictable, adolescent stew of bravado and limited vision?

My students will end up in body bags for sure. I remember how easily I got caught in the same headlights a long time ago.

I think of my son.

IV.

It's been seven weeks now. I think I mentioned that I'm a trauma shrink, right? I teach and write and have a practice on the side. I give speeches about school crisis management. So the New York schools are in crisis, I trained their crisis teams and I want to help. Sent them materials to support the teachers. Wrote a paper outlining strategies. A local crisis team I train was commended for its quick action on the 11th, when the two extra planes were believed to be headed in our direction. I've made calls. I've played cheerleader. I've talked it up—but something isn't moving.

I talked to people at the foundation for which I consult, to the journal for whom I edit, and the New York schools for which I have trained crisis teams in the past. There are no invitations yet. This thing will be a once-in-a-crisis-intervention experience for everyone in the field. It's embarrassing to have to beg.

On my way to and from work, I watch star-spangled Tahoes and Range Rovers as they cut each other off because they've had a bad karma day and I shudder. What do they have to prove? Just whom are they so eager to send to this war? My boy?

V.

It came to me yesterday, after I remembered the drip. The drip that got interrupted by the phone call? Well, I did crawl under the house, and yes, it was a miserable job. The crawl in the dark and spiders gave me some serious flashbacks. And when I felt something slither over my neck and I looked up and saw the hundreds of black widow spider egg sacs all lined up inches over my face, I pretty much freaked. I felt the impact of bodies falling on me from the upper bunks, and the decks lurching, and the big guns started firing again.

But later as I lay there in the silence, I heard the drip again and I thought about things; about how this business isn't Vietnam all over again. It really is different. It seemed there was another jungle involved, though, a place far darker than the one we slowly patrolled each night just offshore. When the gunfire lit that darkness, more leapt out than could ever be put back.

In the peace of that place under my house, I thought about how I had come back from that aborted tour in 1967. I was traumatized, so I built up massive walls. A bunker of my own construction. Why? Because there was so much shit that it was too dangerous to fear. *FEEL! I meant to write "feel," and I wrote "fear." Again, just now, in straightening it out, I began spelling it "fea..."*

Like I said before, I'm a shrink, right.

I know this stuff.

All right, let's start again—But this time, I'm going to listen. I'm a therapist by trade, but you don't have to be Freud to recognize a significant slip. Fear. Fear. Fear. Feel fear. Feel fear. My hands feel leaden on the keyboard. Felt fear, feeling fear. I will feel fear.

> *Some shit happened, all right? It was about being a former medic, turned shell passer, boat driver in helmet and life jacket, on destroyer duty off the DMZ. A sailor—or at least a man acting like one. The maximum*

combat assignment possible without volunteering, sent as punishment for speaking out against the war. Coastal interdiction and artillery support for the firebases. Patrols all day and firing for half the night. Half the rest of the squadron hit by rocket fire from the beach. Two rules: never, ever get off the boat. And never, ever feel.

I am still on O'Brien's Boat.

Some more considerations on my grammar regarding the hypothesis "it is about fear":

It was about fear. It is about fear. It will be about fear.

It was about fear. It is about fear. It may be about fear.

It was about fear—and a lot of other things.

It may be about fear, and a lot of other things.

For me: How do you pay back the world for the life of the medic you should have been when you got busted in rank for speaking out against the war? How do you pay back those guys you could have helped, for the parts of their bodies and souls that were blown away? And how about the guy who became the medic in your place? You can't pay them back—but you try. You have to make every minute count, do impossible things, and you can't enjoy, you can't love, can't allow yourself the passions those who died cannot experience. You build a bunker and hunker down inside and try to figure out how you are going to make the chaos quit. You devote yourself to living a life beyond reproach. You take care of your babies and do everything imaginable to keep them from being blown up.

You take care to protect those who have the bad sense to love you from the rage that threatens to overrun your position every day and every night. You don't feel. You don't feel because it is how you get hurt and how you hurt others.

Sometimes you dream of tidal waves at night.

VI.

This morning I sit at the kitchen table. I've got the coffee and the paper, and I am enjoying the brief calm before waking up the rest of the house. The headlines are grim, but not surprising. Thirty-five firefighters demonstrating at Ground Zero were jailed yesterday after a clash with their brother police officers. The firefighters object to the city reducing the number of body spotters in order to speed the removal of debris. It seems that the firefighters feel that place is a sacred place, that whatever's left of bodies of the 250 or so undiscovered souls should be take priority over the reconstruction of the World Trade Center and the resumption of business as usual. The ominous first sentence of the article reads "In a violent confrontation that revealed the explosive tensions simmering in the city . . ."

I make sure I have my materials to take to the office, even though it's Saturday. After I drop kids off at their respective projects, I'm going to spend the morning pulling together more training material. There's a war on—this time it's not Vietnam, or World War II. It's not about good guys or bad guys or even other countries. It's not about self-protection, or even about making the world safe for capitalist globalization.

Just as the guns before lit up monsters within, our underbelly has been held up to the light. It's right here in each of our hearts. It's about making payments for being as we are. It's about living.

I got the call. I made reservations to fly to New York last night.

The Smell of Angels Burning

All structure fell away in that 9/11 early morning dusk. We gazed frozen with disbelief and then our eyes took it in and we felt our bodies awaken from our toes to our guts to the piled rubble and stink. We forced our brains to function and our bodies to move.

My school crisis team members, psychologists trained to work with small groups, had to go to thirty-two schools. Working solo. Four of the schools were found evacuating through jammed streets, clouds of smoke and dust and falling concrete and dead bodies. No time for grief groups here.

My team members were alone in the chaos. Acres of hurt and confusion and none of the careful plans we'd made and beliefs we held prepared us for anything like this. The communication center had fallen with the second building. Goliath kicked David to the curb. A site principal's last orders were to take his children north into the maelstrom. But there was no more north.

"What should we do?" asked the Chancellor's office and abruptly ended mid-sentence. Looking up at the TV screen set up for monitoring news and watching the tower fall away. A month crawled by to regain that contact, to cut the snarls of red tape and continually fragmenting communications and traumatized decision makers and competing aid agencies and security blockades to get to my team.

> Subway doors open
> nearest station to the site.
> I stand to get off;

passengers look away
as the smell slides on.
The smell. Burnt wire and plastic
bodies and hair.

To sit in that dark early morning basement room to meet with my team. To debrief their worst moments as if that would heal, to calm their recurrent fears as if they were safe, to give them direction when north was missing. To explain why half of them were missing, too afraid to leave home.

Eighty teachers packed in a nice midtown hotel. I speak of healing and hope when a disturbance begins in the middle of the lecture hall. Teachers knocked over chairs while cockroaches poured from a ceiling vent as they fled the construction next door. Hundreds more tiny terrorists falling from the sky.

Xray tech tells me stories
   of endless body bags
      mixed body part masses
         two spines, one tiny, inside
            dark carbon tracks of sentient beings

"Hey! Time to move." A strong hand grabbed her collar from behind and moved her along. She realized she'd been standing for some time staring at the faces. The long bulletin board propped up among sent gifts of teddy bears and flowers dominated the center of the cavernous pier 94 warehouse along the Hudson that had been commandeered by FEMA as a one stop shopping center for victim and family support. Hundreds of faces. Pinned messages: "Have you seen this girl?" "Jeanne, call this number. I'm with friends." "Daddy, please come home."

A child reports: "The birds are on fire."
A teacher saw the angelic iridescence of a billion
tiny shards of glass against the morning sun
another, Satan in the billowing smoke.

Walking up to hotel in Midtown, exhausted from working 7am to 10pm, the only diner available turned out to be signed "Singing Waiters and Waitresses." Professional singers and dancers too had to eat between gigs on stage. Broadway communion with star studded choir.

Agencies fought for position. Outsiders wanted in as much as insiders wanted out—this was the big one, the event to have been to, the resume gem. Firefighters slugged it out with police at the bottom of Ground Zero. FEMA pushed the city around. Homeland Security pushed FEMA around. Psychologists showed up on their own, offering free advice from street corners. Established outfits like the Red Cross elbowed church groups. Preachers and seers shouldered out secular relief. Distribution of service contracts was a clusterfuck and weeks went by as one agency challenged the adequacy of the other to be the one to serve groups in need of support. One teacher told me it was a month before any counselors visited her room.

Informal tests on trauma symptoms showed my team member's scores to exceed those of the staff and students they served. Most of them were in Lower Manhattan when the towers fell, most went into the impact area soon after, and most have been exposed to countless unanticipated and intolerable stories of other's suffering. The stories were radioactive, gifts that kept on giving.

Once in a while an angel would appear, though. You'd know: frazzled look, tired, often frumpy, slight smile perhaps, and a subtle but definite light in the eyes. Often profane. Sometimes smoked and usually drank. Mother Theresa in emergency gear.

Trinity Church with scented candles burning, darker, quieter, less acrid inside. Priest and three choir members rise to packed crowd. Rescuers, workers, a few neighbors gather against heavy equipment dirge just outside in the night. "Let us pray, now for all of us . . ."

Christopher Williams, Th.D.
112 Indian Hill Blvd.
Claremont, CA 91711

January 23, 2002

Dr. Kendall Johnson
c/o FEMA project
Pier 30, Manhattan
New York City

Dear Dr. Johnson,

I suppose I should have waited for you to return from New York; I know you're only there a week or so at a time. There are a couple of things, though, that I thought you might find helpful. You're busy, so I'll keep it short.

You've spoken to me about images being "stuck in your brain" and your needing some kind of "mental floss" to dislodge them. Apt terminology! I realize you've been protecting me from them—as if they are somehow radioactive and that merely sharing them with me would infect me with the same distress you feel. Yet that is my job, and I'll find ways to "floss" as you must. While you're there, it might help to write them down so we can deal with them later.

One last thing, I know that you're taking part in the NYC protests against military retaliation into Iraq on your off time. Just be careful. Those things sometimes turn violent. You may accuse me of taking advantage of my paternal role as clinical supervisor to impose my politics on you, but actually I feel more like your mother.

Take care of yourself,
Dr. Williams, Th.D.

Incident in Harlem

Lecturing at Harlem Horizon hospital, I looked into the fifty or so faces of medical people in the old amphitheater who were looking back at me, waiting. They were emergency room medics, surgical personnel, and crisis workers, unsure that I had any clue about their daily lives on the receiving end of the inner city. What could I—privileged, white, and cocooned—give them that they would find of any use?

After walking the streets, the playground/shooting galleries, the tenement buildings with locked fire escapes, I'd found my way to the Pediatric Orthopedic Surgery Department and met the social worker and the pediatric surgeon who had called me in. They told me of their work, about their endless flow of patients, and their staff. They told me of their mission and projects.

Admission Report
7/16/92

Harlem Hospital
Case 5,458
Tom (NMI) Plank

Here is a young man whose spine did not fuse
whose brain won't recycle its fluid and swells.
His limits leave him open to thugs and gangsters,
to fights and shooting, to wheelchairs and beatings.
His parents have moved on.

He starts ninth grade this year, where looks,
and strength, and status, and abilities are everything.
This boy of twisted body and boundary
embodies everything we fear for ourselves.

Admitted to Harlem Horizon Art Studio program.

Here is the artist
    who picks up a paintbrush
        and opens a world of light.

The social worker for the Pediatric Orthopedic Surgery department walked me around the hospital. Seventeen floors high with elevators so archaic that Donald Trump was said to have visited the place with the intention of fixing the elevators to eliminate the bottlenecks in the corridors. They had been disappointed when he announced that the elevators would be too expensive to fix.

Dr. Barbara Barlow, Chief of Pediatric Surgery had made time to speak with me about a consultation report I made after reviewing their Injury Prevention Program. They planned to teach street first aid to neighborhood kids and wanted to run the curriculum by me to determine if exposure to the training scenarios would cause the children to be traumatized. In other words, how do you gently teach a kid that he or she shouldn't pull a knife out of someone who'd been stabbed? How do you teach safe needle disposal so that they can safely police up the shooting galleries that pass as playgrounds? How to hold someone's intestines in when they've fallen from a tenement window without bars and onto a fence topped with spear points?

I sat on the top floor of the hospital in the Horizon Art Center, talking to Bill Richards, the director. The center occupies a large room with long tables forming a rectangular work area in the center and a set of upright easels scattered around the edges. Once artists have proven they are serious, they graduate from the group tables to the single workstations. Bill tells me about the effectiveness of his program, the enchantment of art, and how it almost magically promotes healing. He offered his story of Jericho, his famous success.

Jericho had suffered a debilitating injury on the streets and had been confined to a wheelchair. His progress toward recovery had plateaued for months, and Jericho had become despondent. Upon entering the art program, he had taken an interest in painting and had developed his own characteristic style. Jericho's work had gotten him some notice and into one of the galleries downtown.

Bill told me how Jericho would always begin paintings at the bottom of the painting and work his way gradually to the top. One day Bill started him on a new canvas, larger than his customary size. Bill described how Jericho had mixed a beautiful cobalt blue, his favorite hue for the sky and was approaching the top of the dark building cityscape. Jericho had to reach to complete it. As he strained ever higher to the unaccustomed large canvas he couldn't reach high enough. So he stood up to complete the painting.

* * *

It was time for me to begin my presentation down in the hospital amphitheater. We waited for the elevator down to the second floor. I had been called there to address the effects of working closely with all that the streets could bring in, the pointless deaths, the suffering: the layers of anguish they absorbed daily. I was to tell them about how this outer mess could trigger their morass within, how they could reach inside for strength to help them hurt less and deliver more. And they were going to tell me a few things as well.

They told me their stories of needless deaths, of children sold and babies baked in ovens by their drug-addled parents, of street corner executions by burning tire necklacing. You couldn't work at Harlem Hospital without living the images.

By noon we had explored the felt aspects of their work, and I was depleted. I withdrew to a private office to eat alone and try to find the energy I needed to go on, to do what I was supposed to be teaching them to do. Knowing I needed the energy, I forced down a sandwich, ate half an apple, then pushed aside the plate and laid my head on the table, falling into a half-sleep. Feeling despair at the task ahead, I longed for some sort of direction. My thoughts swirled unproductively, and then a memory arose.

"You are sitting by the water with someone," suggests the guide who leads us into dreamtime. Here is the water fountain in the San Diego Mission, looking past to the surrounding mountains, the flowers arranged around the fountain. The adobe fountain cascades crystalline water in an arc, the breeze blows the mist into patterns of silver raindrops that fall onto delicate skin. Someone sits next to me. A burro stands on the other side of the fountain. On its back a pack frame holds quadriplegic's bracing, the kind that supports a person under the shoulders and around the hips, and extends down the thighs to hold just above the knees.

It was at a workshop I attended a year or so ago, hosted by a retreat center. After the imagery we talked about its meaning. Supports that help but keep us dependent. Then in another session:

"You will meet God," suggests the guide who leads us back into dreamtime. The old ranch house is pleasantly ramshackle, and the party seems to be picking up. My father—already deceased by a half decade—is there and we take bets as to who can race out to the well and back first. Encouraged by shouting revelers we dash through the back door, across the yard past chickens, touch the pump. When we do oil rigs hit oil and we are black and smelling with the oil rain. Back inside I notice a young man with shoulder length black hair. He is smiles with the merriment and shakes my hand. My world shimmers into centuries.

I recall several similar encounters over the subsequent year; the same young man, the youthfulness and vitality. I've always been left breathless by his gaze, his forthrightness.

"God will give you something," suggests the guide who leads us into dreamtime. Firewood pops sparks swirling into the still night sky peppered with stray stars and galaxies slowly fading with faint promise of dawn. Juniper mixes with sage smoke, mixes with the breeze and I crouch waiting in the cold by the fire. Into the circle walks a man, Bedouin robes and black shoulder length hair frames piercing eyes dark as the overhead sky. Looking into mine he offers an onyx spear tipped with gold. He looks into me for days, nods, then turns abruptly leaving the procession below that marches toward some lasting battle. I hold the spear and watch the sky lighten, waiting.

The meaning was clear; it was to be used in my own battles. In the days that followed I deployed it as I found uses for it, sometimes as hypnotic image shared with clients, sometimes kept to myself, sometimes talking about it, several times in the weeks to come. Then came Sally.

Sally is racked with spinal cancer pain that medicine can't touch without costing her the few days that remain with her family. She asks for my help, as I know a hypnotic protocol helpful with pain. We work there in the living room by the fire as her family waits in the next room. In the midst of Sally's dream, I reach for the onyx spear. "Your family is strong and ready" I suggest. I plunge its golden tip past her chest and into the heart of the pain. Her gasp startles both of us. Later, pain moderated, she lives out her last few weeks unimpeded, able to communicate with her family and help them through the process of her parting.

In my mind, I find myself back in the amphitheater, looking up at the faces of the medics and therapists of Harlem Hospital waiting expectantly. This time I sense I have something they need. I take up my spear and gently touch each, systematically, one after the other, allowing the energy I had felt before flow through the spear. I serve as a conduit, an instrument carrying a current I can feel but do not understand.

As I come to each of them I am able to recall their faces. I sense their need and feel each of them grow warm. And just as I finish touching the very last person with the spear I am awoken by a knock at the door.

"The group has reassembled from lunch, Doctor. It's time to begin . . ."

Supervisory Verbatim #14

Being Enough

Dr. Williams sat back in his chair, seeming to get comfort-able. I had the distinct impression he was coiling to strike. I guess I was feeling vulnerable, but I didn't know why.

"Back from another one?" he asked pleasantly. "Anything you'd like to report?"

"Just got back from Harlem. I spoke at the hospital. It was interesting, but some weird stuff happened."

"How so?"

I stayed with it. "I'm working clinically, right? So something happened I can't explain."

Williams smiled ironically. "There's not much that happens that I can explain anymore."

"So there I was at Harlem Hospital doing a presentation to ER, pediatric surgery, and their crisis team. It was tough and by the time I got through the morning I was so tired I didn't think I could do the afternoon simulations. At lunch I caught a quick nap and had this vision in which I used a magic spear to touch each of the participants' hearts. When I went back into the auditorium I gave the best presentation I've ever done."

"So you think you worked some magic? What's the problem with that?"

I said, quietly, "The problem is that I don't know if I can do it again."

"You really got a charge out of it, didn't you?"

"It was crazy. I totally get high from it and I want to do it again," I smiled. "What's wrong with that?"

"Because it's so addictive. You say its a rush, you get pumped. You're playing Hero."

"That's all true," I had to admit. "Satisfying—like nothing else. Hell, it's my nirvana."

"But it leads to problems, right? That's the problem with the 'Hero' thing. We buy into the myth that being Hero completes us, makes us worth loving, gets us acclaim. We're the warriors and workers, brave and bold. We sacrifice ourselves to the fight. But when we go into battle mode, we get callous to each other and mostly to ourselves. We compartmentalize, we shut down, we don't feel. And we bring the distance home."

"Well, I guess." I thought for a moment about childhood, about the days I spent in the lemon grove growing up, where each of the trees was a dragon to be slain, a warship to be sailed, or a fortress to be defended. How my father would tell me to stop bellyaching, how he'd caution me not to cry.

Dr. Williams was on a roll. "We're trained to push ourselves beyond what's healthy, to want to attain that rare pearl—acceptance. Our culture teaches us that message through its agents: its entertainment and schools, its parents, and especially our fathers. We end up naive choirboys going forth armed with notions of honor and excellence, our heads full of glory, walking into a fractured and damaged world that chews us up. And all this time what we are really looking for is self-acceptance."

"And then," I said, "we turn around and bring all that pain home to our families."

"Yes. We become that world. Then we have to park in some therapist's office and try to figure out where we went so badly off track, how we got so fractured and damaged."

"But what is the right track? How do we un-fracture ourselves." I asked.

Williams looked at me. "That's the whole point. You *are already* on the right track."

Healing Dr. Morella Joseph

If you stand on the very top of the highest cliff in front of the lighthouse on the southernmost tip of the Island of St. Lucia and look south toward Venezuela, maybe 200 miles away, you will notice the turbulent meeting ground of lighter turquoise Caribbean Sea on your right, and the heavier indigo Atlantic ocean on your left. This sometimes-broken line of colliding wind, wave, and temperature patterns leaves a foam wake snaking south as far as you can see.

The high school principal, Dr. Morella Joseph, had been tormented by fears and clinical grade startle reactions for the four months following a brutal attack by two students that had almost cost her her life. Once stabilized, she fled to her family, who lived in England. She had only returned for the hearing, which would take place in several days. She was still shaken, unable to relax or focus. She had heart palpitations and flashbacks when anything reminded her of her ordeal. She woke at night with terrifying nightmares of being accosted by obscure figures with large knives. Sister Des Lourdes hoped that I could help.

I had one chance to work with this woman, and my schedule could hardly afford that one visit. I'd pumped Sister Des Lourdes for background information as we rode up the mountain, while we bumped through the deep potholes and shallow streams and fought slipping off the muddy, uneven road into the underbrush. She told me a story of Morella Joseph, of a girl who grew up poor in Vieux Fort, who somehow fought her way to Jamaica to study and put herself through the University there to eventually win a doctorate in Education. The Sister told me how Morella, then with a doctorate, had returned to St. Lucia to teach, and then became the principal of the high school, never again felt at home with her people. Even her professional colleagues were intimidated by her. Her district superintendent was far less educated than she, and even the people in the Ministry of Education in Castries couldn't cope with her knowledge and determination.

"Why?" I asked.

"Because in our country, women must not be bold, or forceful."

"With her education, could she not become a leader?"

Sister Des Lourdes thought for a moment. "St. Lucians have high rates of alcohol abuse and domestic violence. The culture demands that men be taken more seriously than women. There is much fear among women not to antagonize men. In the same way, there is a fear among men not to appear weak."

"So she can't expect to climb further than high school principal?" I asked. "She does have a doctorate."

"Dr. Morella Joseph would make a brilliant Minister of Education. But here it is highly unlikely—and now this, being the victim of a crime. She isn't sure she can even bring herself to return to the high school."

*   *   *

When we arrived, we talked with Dr. Joseph in her house in the hills overlooking Vieux Fort. Sister Des Lourdes waited in the kitchen, working on a report in her brief time away from the constant distractions of the hospital. It was quiet in this place. How I had been talked into being part of a training mission in a Catholic hospital still confused me. I was clear though, that as a shrink specializing with trauma, I should try to help this woman. I wasn't a religious believer—and even if I had been, the nature of the story she told would certainly have challenged my faith—but this wasn't about choosing sides. The lady needed whatever help I could bring.

Dr. Morella Joseph could scarcely maintain eye contact with me. She spoke of her inability to relax and her loss of concentration, of her confusion about why she had been attacked, and her fears for her future and returning to work. She was worried about her 16-year-old son, Storm, who was himself unable to return to the same school, partly for fear of harassment and partly because of peer pressure for him to exact revenge. That was something he didn't want, but that was the custom in St. Lucia.

She told us that she was determined to take advantage of this chance to work on her fears so that she could return to her work at the school. After discussing her various symptoms— fear of reoccurance of an attack being the worst—we decided to go ahead with an approach I knew which would work to desensitize her fear as well as her memories. Due to the severity of her intrusive memories and reactions, I decided to mix my approach, starting first with a standard review of the incident to identify particularly painful images that evoked her fearful reactions. It turned out she had plenty to tell.

*　　*　　*

On the day of the attack Dr. Mirella Joseph was preoccupied with getting an athletic team off for a match in Castries. Dr. Joseph had returned to make a phone call from her small office on the second floor of classrooms, and she had paid little attention to the two seventeen-year-old boys who approached her asking for change for a large bill. Not questioning why they were not in class, she bent down to reach for her purse, and felt a sharp stinging blow to the side of her head. A sudden shower rained down over her hands and purse. The warm, sticky blood flowed over her neck and shoulders and she was sickened by the smell of it. Regaining her feet, she warded off two more blows, sustaining deep cuts to her hands and forearms. By this time she realized that her assailant was wielding a cutlass, or machete.

The large boy who had used the cutlass on her then turned to pull closed the door, trapping her inside the small office. The other boy, shocked at the ferocity of the attack, stood staring at her, transfixed, merely watching. Morella Joseph knew that the door sometimes locked itself from the outside accidentally, and also knew that if the boys managed to lock her in, she would die.

Dr. Morella Joseph put her head down and charged the door, shoving the larger attacker off balance. Staggering out of the office, she ran down the hall and took refuge in a classroom, and yelled for the teacher to call security. When the assailants fled, she was helped down the stairs by teachers and into a van. Dr. Morella Joseph, bleeding from her wounds, was driven through the crowded streets to St. Judes Hospital as she lay in the back seat.

*   *   *

Arriving at St. Judes, she got out of the van and, still holding her head together to staunch the flow of blood, ran into the outpatient clinic. She pushed aside stunned onlookers and climbed up onto the examination table. This act galvanized the shocked staff into action. They fought to clamp off the bleeding veins and eventually placed stitches both inside and outside the wounds.

"They wrapped up my head and pushed me through the halls on a gurney to get X-rays."

"You remember all this?" I asked.

"Oh yes, Doctor," she said. "I knew I had to stay awake to stay alive."

Complicating hospital operations was the fact that people all over Vieux Fort were hearing that the principal had been attacked. People dropped their tools, left their work, and found their way to St. Judes. The public transport vans discharged load after load of islanders at the hospital gates. A crowd of hundreds had amassed, many from as far away as Castries, an hour and a half to the north. Two governmental ministers arrived. The crowd pressed in the hallways and the security force was unable to push them back. Dr. Morella Joseph had to be pushed through a labyrinth of inner passages to avoid the crowd in order to get to X-ray and the lab. Later, as she was resting in her recovery room, the crowd was allowed to come into the room in groups of five to express their wishes for her recovery. Tears streamed down their faces as they left.

*　　*　　*

There was no shortage of painful images in her account. She told me of how difficult it was to keep going, how frustrating it was to push through the crowds of people in shock, how the nurses were holding her hands and crying for her. "I had no idea I meant anything to all these people, that they even knew who I was."

We worked on. I helped her identify the exaggerated feelings and the physical symptoms that were associated with those images. We struggled to understand what the experiences—and reactions—meant in terms of her changing concept of herself and of the world. We tried to make sense of her future. Once we had these images and connections laid out, we began using a variety of approaches to neutralize their effects. It was complicated, but the process bore fruit. We peeled away layer after layer of hurt.

"Morella," I exclaimed at one point, "you must mean much to these people, even if they don't understand all you do for them."

"I just can't leave them," she reflected. "not just the girls, but the boys, too."

We systematically visited the images, the memories, dreams, nightmares and daytime hauntings, one at a time, until each was softened and made manageable. The memories of the attack, the pain and the fear of death were replaced by memories of the concern of the people who loved her.

Near the the end of our work together, in the late afternoon light, I held one of her hands while she held her head, her other hand near the scars. Suddenly, she sat up and took a deep breath, much like one would when surfacing after being too deep in water too long.

"Oh, Doctor!" she gasped. "I am alive!" Her skin color had returned. Her eyes danced about as if she had just noticed her surroundings. She smiled broadly, "I am alive!"

*　　*　　*

As we finished our session we spoke of her work here on the island and how it was unfinished. In the past weeks, due to her fears, self-doubt, and uncertainties she'd been thinking of another line of work or even of moving as far away as England. Now she was aware that her staff and students needed her back, that her work on the island was important. Something was left undone, I realized, unsaid.

I went out and found Sister Des Lourdes working on her charts and brought her back to the room. "Sister," I began. "This woman has been realizing how important her work is here in St. Lucia. She no longer sees the scars she bears on her head as points of shame. In fact those scars may be very important to her work in the years to come."

Sister Des Lourdes smiled at Dr. Morella Joseph and said, "They are painful now, but they may bring you great joy, and they may give you great insight and grant wisdom to those whom you touch."

"We can't understand now what all these scars will bring," I added, "but we need to bless these marks, to make them sacred. Sister, could you pray for this woman, to bless her scars and her life?"

And the sweet Sister from Trinidad held Dr. Morella Joseph in her arms, gently laid her hands upon Morella's wounds, and in her lovely sing-song voice said a prayer of "blessin." And Dr.

Morella Joseph relaxed into the Sister's arms, and a smile of radiant peace moved across her face.

*   *   *

After we drove down the mountain and got back into town, Sister Des Lourdes stopped the car in a less-frequented, more industrial area of Vieux Fort near the waterfront. We got out, and I followed her up a narrow street, gradually becoming aware of an indefinable music just out of hearing. She opened the large wooden door in the back of a nondescript building and led me up the tall stairs. The music grew louder, more sweet and familiar.

"I thought you might like to see this," she smiled, and opened the door at the top of the stairs to the choir practice of a steel drum choir.

I'd always thought of steel drumming as part of a secular party scene, just like I thought of the church as part of the po-litical establishment. As we listened to the rolling sound of steel drums moving from calypso rhythm to an emerging "Nearer My God to Thee" melody. Sister Des Lourdes nodded out the tall window, through which I could make out the mountain-ous top of the high cliff with its *Moule a Chique* lighthouse. It is from there I stood and looked south and saw the turbulent, serpentine seam where the warm turquoise waters of the Ca-ribbean met and after much roiling merged with the cooler, indigo waters of the deeper sea.

Supervisory Verbatim #14

Storms

Dr. Williams' office sanctuary beckoned on this rainy afternoon, and I had spent many helpful afternoons here. Christopher Williams, Th.D. had a storied background as truck driver and Episcopal Priest prior to clinical training that I felt deepened his understanding of the situations I shared from my work as a psychological consultant to large incident crisis management. We'd review the incidents I'd been involved in since the last visit and sort out my reactions to the incidents and implications we could draw for future events. There was no reason to suspect otherwise today. It began to rain as we sat down to talk.

"So, what parts of yourself have you been avoiding, flying like you do around the countryside chasing fires and whatever else you get yourself into?"

Then Dr. Williams inquired about my recent work in the Caribbean Island of St. Lucia. While my main work was providing training in trauma management to St. Jude Hospital, I'd been asked to work with a high school principal who'd been attacked by two students who had slashed her with machetes. I found the whole business disturbing.

"Of course. Machetes are disturbing," Dr. Williams commented.

"But it was more than the violence, which was bad enough. A nun had gotten involved with the session and I'd gotten deeper than I expected and seemed to be part of something bigger. It felt like I'd been a part of an actual healing. It reminded me of

Harlem where something else—bigger than just me—was in play. Strange."

"Ethereal?"

"Yeah, a little like playing with things way above my pay grade. I'm not sure what it all means. And last night I had this vivid dream that you feature in, and I wondered if I could share it with you and maybe we could talk it through?"

"Sure. Sounds like fun." We could hear the thunder roll outside and the rain getting harder.

I told Williams that the dream had taken place in a supervision session. While I was talking about incidents, my supervisor had been going through the motions of a religious ceremony.

"It was like the things I was saying about the incidents or about the people I was dealing with were all secondary to the ritual he was going through with me. It was almost like a communion ceremony," I said.

"Interesting," Williams said. "What sense did you make of it?"

"Not much. It seemed unreal—his going through the ritual seemed much more important than giving me insight into the incident I was trying to tell him about."

"Maybe the dream was telling you something. Something about your work out there."

"Like?" I knew what was coming, but I still felt like a deer to his headlights.

"Were you working deeply with the woman who was attacked? Psychologically?"

"I explored what had happened, then used hypnosis. We did go deep."

"Anything unexpected happen?"

I thought for a moment. "Yes, it did, actually. I sensed that we'd reached a point where we were working at accepting what had happened. We were talking about valuing her scars, the outward leftovers from the attack, as important keys to her work in the future. Because she was Catholic, I brought her friend, Sister Des Lourdes, the nun who had brought me to the hospital, into the room. The sister blessed the scars to reinforce their importance and worth in the future."

"An external reinforcement to the lesson?" Williams suggested.

"And internal—it was important to her."

"And to you?" he gently probed.

"Something about the experience was compelling. It was almost spooky."

"Interesting choice of words."

"Spooky?" I wondered.

"And 'compelling' both," said Williams. "I'm wondering why? If you had a similar experience in Harlem and then the one here, what's keeping you from accepting those experiences as real. Why can't you do what you are prescribing to the principal—use the scars, use all that you know?"

"But that's the problem. I don't know." I was remembering something. "When I was a kid, maybe in first grade, my parents dressed up as cannibals."

William's eyebrows raised.

"It was Halloween and there was a parade. They wore body suits, make up, carried spears. We walked in the school parade. It was the 50s and politically appalling, but they really got into it. Later, when we went home—we lived on a lemon ranch— we discovered that coyotes had broken into the enclosure we kept ducks in and slaughtered them. Bloody white feathers and intestines against the darkness. I had loved those ducks."

"That is frightening. Any other associations with dark forces?"

I realized another connection. "On my first year with the Forest Service we responded to a vehicle over the side above a reservoir. It was my first multi-casualty and they were kids my age out partying. Halloween night, again. I hate Halloween. Middle of the night, dust was roiling from our climbing up the side of the hill into the blinding bright lights from the engine. The girl was screaming in pain as we tried to keep her stretcher steady, inches from my face. Rocks kept getting kicked loose and flying by our heads out of the glare. Then she was silent. She died because we couldn't keep the stretcher still enough going up that nearly vertical road cut. When we got to the top a hand reached down out of the glare to help me up and over the top. It was covered with a white glove. When I pulled myself up I was looking into the face of a guy wearing a death costume. His face was white. Spooky."

"No wonder you don't like things you can't control. Chaos."

"I remember sliding the stretcher with her body into the ambulance and a girl in another stretcher reaching down and asking, 'How's Cathy? How's my sister?' and I turned away and got sick."

"So when you say, 'spooky' you really do mean spooky. Strobe-light memories set in deep and still disturbing. Look, you see the parallel, don't you, between you touching on the mysterious in your work, and then you avoiding the spiritual dimension because it's out of your control?"

I saw connection but wasn't sure I wanted to go there. "I know you're going to say that we should be able to accept and reclaim worrisome parts of ourselves. It's good theory, at least in principle." I shook my head. "Easier said than done."

"We still have some work to do," agreed Dr. Williams. "The thing to hold on to, though, is trusting yourself enough to do what you came here to do."

A Walk in the Woods

The 3.4-mile out-and-back Tokopah Falls trail leads through a glacial valley, climbs initially under a canopy of pine and fir, through meadows and creek-crossings, and past "glacial erratics" (irregularly shaped boulders dropped millenia ago by glaciers.) The trail eventually climbs steep granite slopes and winds through huge rocks, leading to the base of the falls. Here the Marble Fork of the Kaweah River falls some 1,200 feet over a series of steep cascades.

> Climbing
> trail leads us up; forgetting that
> our incandescent star
> hides the darkness
> for now.
>
> Up here
> trees fall away,
> Glacial Erratics find
> their way down canyon toward the sea
> beyond.

I.

The deep vein thrombosis broke loose as I reached the top of the trail out of Lodgepole campground that leads to Tokopah Falls, but I hadn't figured it out yet. The resulting embolism passed through my heart, splitting into two halves at the juncture, and lodged in both lungs. By all rights, according to the docs later, I should have died right then.

Instead, starving for oxygen at only 6,500 feet, I just needed badly to sit down. The shade of an overhanging ledge beckoned. I sat. Since I was on a solo photo shoot for my friend's book, I shot what I could from a sitting position. Drank some water. Then, when sitting was too much work, I lay down. As I looked up, surreal deep blue sky seemed to pull beyond the overhang. Empty sky, so rich, tiny bird high above. It was as if I floated, like that bird, drifting gently. I did like the forest, especially up high. Coming down just seemed like so much work. Lying down looking up felt right, almost a bed at home. The mountains had been home for me since I was much younger, working on a fire crew in Southern California, sometimes good and sometimes not. Fun to remember.

II.
Dream #1, 1964

If you drive ten miles up the San Gabriel Canyon Road out of Azusa, you'll come to the East Fork bridge. Turn right and continue up past the county prison Camp 14, past Shady Grove campground and a general store where the Hell's Angels like to come up and party, and even past the turnoff to the Glendora Mountain Road. Then, after the road turns north past the Cattle Canyon bridge, you'll see the East Fork Ranger Station up to the right, near the end. That's where I worked.

The station boasts a fire engine, its crew of four, a patrol truck, and a patrol officer whose sworn duty it is to enforce Forest laws and regulations. While the patrolman is not properly part of the engine crew, he nevertheless, because of the isolation of the station and the connection between forest crimes and fire danger, is definitely a functional member. Dave Smith could not be ignored.

And Dave took his job very seriously. His uniform was always cleaned and pressed, never mind the fact that the pants—

due to the physical nature of much of his work—were green Levi's. His top-of-the-line White Smokejumper boots were always properly brushed and greased, and he lit up his Pall Mall reds with a Zippo with Smokey Bear's face emblazoned on the side. Dave got his flattop haircut closely trimmed on shopping expeditions downtown twice a month. Dave was squared away. His dream was to get out of the Forest Service and move down the hill. He wanted to sign on to the Azusa Fire Department and drive one of their big American LaFrance engines, work regular hours, and make bank.

It's not like Dave was obsessed with money. He wasn't. Nor did he long for big city life. It's just that his priorities were getting rearranged by the fact that his wife had given birth to twins last year and was beginning to worry a lot about Dave being stuck 45 minutes on a road subject to mud and rock slide. It was becoming clear to her, and thus clearer to Dave, that getting to school, doctors, shopping, and friends was becoming a problem. She wasn't happy. And when she wasn't, it wasn't long before Dave wasn't happy.

On the other hand, Dave did like station life. While a little slow in terms of action, he wasn't mired down in project work like the fire crew between their infrequent rolls. When they were sifting dirt for the new barracks lawn, breaking out paint brushes for the campground privy, or cutting the new firebreak 300 feet up the hill behind the station under the 100 degree heat, Dave would pull out of the station "on patrol" to walk the stream beds in the shade, or have a beer down at Shady Grove with the proprietor while they discussed the new hazard mitigation regs. Dave always dutifully left his outside speaker turned on so that conversations would be punctuated by the various squawks and bleeps of radio traffic. It gave it all a sense of gravity and impending action.

Dave did enjoy the first hour or so spent in the station office sipping coffee and smoking with the fire engine captain after the crew had finished their physical training, washed and warmed up the engine, and were sweeping out the office under his and the captain's helpful eye. Dave considered this valuable "pre-planning" time.

Every now and then the morning's somnambulance was broken by some inconsiderate civilian racing up the station driveway, horn blowing, skidding to a stop and frantically searching for the office while Dave and the captain calmly regarded him out of the office window and sipped their coffee. This wasn't a deliberate negligence of duty; it probably was not a genuine emergency, and if it were they probably wouldn't be able to finish their coffee. This was to be such a morning.

A rather senior citizen broke into their office begging for help. "Well, fellers," he sputtered with a pronounced lisp and obvious determination to endure whatever humiliation was necessary to get help, "I was down at the picnic area, takin' a leak in the outhouse, you know...," He paused, waiting for Dave or the captain to nod encouragement. They didn't, but rather fixed him with their most non-committal gaze. "I sneezed! Couldn't help it." The captain's coffee cup stopped mid-sip and Dave froze in the middle of taking a drag on his Pall Mall. The man continued: "My teeth . . . my teeth shot right out of my mouth and down the crapper." The outhouse in question was a non-flushing pit toilet. He held his head back and his mouth open to demonstrate the missing upper plate.

Dave exhaled and the captain lowered his cup. Sometimes the Muse falls upon unlikely fields. After they glanced at each other for a minute, the captain turned to the junior crewman and with the straightest face announced: "Tell Cooper to fire up the engine. We've got a roll."

The crewman darted out of the office, called to Coop and John, and hauled on the chain pulley to raise the great garage door in a clatter of dust. The engine started and pulled out into the driveway and waited with red lights flashing. The siren wailed, calling the crew to saddle up and belt down while Cooper was calling in to dispatch: "Engine 2-8 responding to a civilian assist at the Burro Flats picnic area." Dave followed the Captain into the shop to fashion a small wire basket on the end of an eight foot long pole. They loaded it on top of the engine's hose rack and the crew held it in place and locked up the station. First the patrol truck and then the engine pulled out of the driveway and rolled down the canyon in full red light and siren, a Code-3 emergency response.

A group of on-lookers gathered in the picnic area as the emergency vehicles slid to a dusty stop. Watermelons, beer, illegal barbecues, and crying babies were forgotten in the excitement, as the firefighters in full gear responded to the captain's crisp order: "All right; Drill #7 on the outhouse! Look sharp, people!" The junior crewman nearly fell over himself trying to look sharp climbing off the raised crew seat armed with the scoop basket.

Just then the captain froze. A portly middle-aged gentleman had just entered the outhouse in question, the roll of toilet paper in his hand giving all indication that he might be a while. "Hold it right there, partner!" the captain bellowed, banging on the locked door with the butt of his No. 3 Heavy Duty Ray-O-Vac flashlight. "This is the US Forest Service! With the power vested in me by the Senior Forester, I order you to stop what you're doing immediately and come out of there!" The man's look of resentment and frustration changed to confusion as he looked into the determined eyes of five firefighters in hard hats and gloves carrying a long pole between them. "Out of the way" came the command, as the captain pushed by followed by the pole-wielding crewman.

Dave's outside speaker crackled. "Dispatch, Patrol 2-8. We are 10-8 at Burro Flats. Situation is contained. Estimate 10 minutes." He listened to the bumps and scrapings going on inside the crowded outhouse, and observed the crowd of largely overweight and under-attractive Looky-Lu's gathered around the unfolding drama. He lit a cigarette and tried to focus on the smell of the smoke, reflecting upon his hard-won insight:

the world breaks down into two kinds of people, emergency personnel and assholes. Dave wasn't all that convinced about the emergency folks, either.

Finally, the captain emerged from the crapper, holding over his head a small object discreetly wrapped in toilet paper. The crowd applauded. As the old man thankfully received his expensive if somewhat rank upper plate, the captain announced that the old man had better boil it for at least 12 minutes before using it again. The captain was obviously pleased with himself; not just for the successful outcome, but for the grace and wit with which the operation had been carried out.

As they pulled out of the campground, the crew was pleased to hear the crowd applaud again and to hear Dave call it in: "Dispatch, Engine 2-8 is 10-19 back to station; Patrol 2-8 is 10-8 to Shady Grove, patrol." Dave figured it was time to swing by the campground and take a look at things, and then stop at the store and talk some more about those new regulations over something cold to drink.

III

I am thirsty. Maybe I slept on that rock by the falls, I'm not sure. I realized I was looking straight up at that bird again, but it now seems bigger. I can see now it is a turkey vulture circling lazily a couple of hundred feet overhead. His feathers catch the morning sun, shifting patterns of gold and shadow as his flight pattern shifts from figure eights to slower circles above me. It takes me some time to realize that the object of his growing interest is me.

It's funny how rocks can seem soft and inviting; how sometimes you just want to merge with it all and let things take their own course and you with it. To sleep, perhaps, to let things go. Maybe some time to fly.

IV
Dream #2, 1964

Dave pulled into the Shady Grove campground. 10 or so private campsites meandered along the riverbed below the store. While the campsites weren't Forest Service, they presented a threat of fire or injury so Dave made a practice of cruising through once or twice a day to fly the colors, check on things, and win some hearts and minds. Besides, the owner welcomed his presence, and usually they had a cold beer afterwards, sitting on the picnic table overlooking the river.

It was still early so the canyon wasn't busy yet. This was the time of day he could stay up here forever. By noon it would be full of urban refugees, all seeking to be free. There would be plenty to patrol for then, with the illegal campfires, accidents, and occasional fight. But not yet.

He swung through the campground and looked over the stream bottom for trash. He had just about made it through when he noticed the faded white, old model Ford Falcon parked a little way away from the outhouses. He couldn't figure out at first what it was that didn't look right. Then he noticed the hose.

It appeared to be a washing machine outlet hose, maybe an inch and a half in diameter, running from underneath the back end of the car up, and back into a back window. "Oh, man . . ." muttered Dave as he flipped on his emergency lights and accelerated toward the car. Sort of silly, he thought self-consciously. Who are the lights for, anyway?

Pulling up beside the car, Dave slipped out of his patrol truck and ran over to the driver's side. Within sat a large man, Caucasian although it was hard to tell because of the splotchy red and gray coloring of the swollen skin. The man's half shut eyes would be staring ahead, were they not glazed over. Dave couldn't help noticing the walrus mustache and the hands. They were resting on his lap, palms up with the middle fingers touching the opposing thumb.   But he was obviously beyond meditation. Dave beat on the car windows and top with his hands, getting no response. The man's face was mostly gray, the hands mostly red. The blood was pooling into the lower extremities and Dave guessed he'd been dead for several hours.

"Dispatch, Patrol 2-8."

"This is Dispatch, 2-8."

"Dispatch, I've got a completed suicide, in the victim's car."

"2-8, what is your 10-20?"

"Dispatch, my 10-20 is the Shady Oaks campground, East Fork. Dispatch, should I break a window?"

"2-8, is the car engine running?"

"That's a negative, Dispatch. The engine is no longer running, nor is the hood hot. Victim is unresponsive and appears to have been dead a while."

The radio squawks and crackles while the dispatcher talked with someone else. "Negative on breaking in, 2-8. Ambulance, Engine 2-8 and Sheriff en route, ETA 20 minutes. Secure and await assistance."

"10-4, Dispatch. Patrol 2-8 out."

Dave sat silently in his truck. Mercifully, no civilians had happened by yet to view the scene; once that started it would be a circus. Dave grabbed his thermos, turned his radio to the outside speaker, got out and walked over to the picnic table and sat down to await reinforcements. The forest was still, apart from the birds. The idle of the patrol truck served to mask whatever smells might emanate from the car.

It had all been quite intentional. The hose was taped in place in the exhaust and the business end fit snugly into the spider web shatter-patterned hole in the right rear window. It too was reinforced and sealed by duct tape. Man's best friend——duct tape, Dave mused. Never let you down. The car was old and showed hard mileage. Dave's eyes fell on a fading bumper sticker. "One Day at a Time" it read in church/gothic print. Oh shit, he thought, Alcoholics Anonymous.

Dave put down his coffee and walked over to the car. The body was—the man had been—overweight and needed a haircut. The clothes were maybe Kmart at best. The car had that lived-in look. Laundry baskets, a box of food, and several shirts on hangers filled the front seat and floor in the back. A sleeping bag and pillow were on the back seat along with some papers and a beat-up attaché case. Propped up on the dashboard were several pictures of children and a woman. One of the pictures had him in it, thinner and younger. The backyard was pretty. Obviously happier times. There were several objects that must have held some significance; a couple of religious icons adorned the mirror and an old military service medal, a purple heart, had been placed among the pictures.

Dave went back to his coffee. A pretty bleak picture, all in all. It didn't take a rocket scientist to read it as a broken life. One fucking day at a time. The addicts equivalent of "Have a Nice Day." How many days had he himself woken up wondering if the effort was worth it? How many meetings?

The anger came easily, if unexpectedly. "You stupid son of a bitch," he began aloud, throwing a pine cone at the car. Dave stopped when he became aware of someone standing behind him. Dave looked around to see an older fellow, perhaps 60, with long gray hair and a beard. He wore mountain clothes—dungarees and flannel—and had a funny expression in his eyes, which Dave couldn't place. Lively, maybe.

"What happened?" the man asked simply.

"Suicide, most likely," Dave wondered how long the guy had been there. "Found him this way."

"Davenport," the man stuck out his hand. "Michael Davenport."

"Oh, yeah." Dave recognized the guy. "You live up in the end cabin up Fish Creek. We've never met. I'm Dave Smith."

"You've left messages on my door."

"Notices. You're behind on your hazard reduction." Dave smiled. "We can't get there on time to keep your home from burning down if you let the weeds grow up to your walls."

"Point taken." Michael's eye's twinkled. "So, what about this guy?"

"Pretty straightforward. Asphyxiation. I'm not an investigator, but I don't see any signs of struggle."

"We all struggle, my friend," Michael replied. "some of us more than others. You always throw pine cones at dead people? Yell at them?" Dave looked at him. "What's the buy-in?" Michael persisted. Dave wondered if he would have to cordon off the area.

"Occupational hazard," Michael ventured. "I've seen a lot of it up here. Not Forest Service, necessarily. Mid-life crisis, I guess, seeing too much. Folks work so long and get tired of it all. Lose touch with themselves and everybody else. Add that to your *Wilderness Protection Act*."

"What?"

"Write in a clause protecting older aged *Homo Sapiens*; we're an endangered species."

Dave couldn't help laughing. "You know, I was really pissed off at him. Maybe a little jealous."

Michael thought for a moment. "How long do we have until the Cavalry arrives? How 'bout we send this guy off proud?" He walked past the car and into the brush, prowled around for moment, and came back tying some sprigs of dried sage together with some string he found in his pocket. "Native Americans burn this stuff to purify the air and clear out evil spirits. Join me."

Dave started to caution him about fires outside of stoves, but restrained himself. "What are you fixing to do?"

"Let's do a chant to the dead that I learned," and without waiting for a reply, began a simple, repetitive song with a full and resonant voice. Dave wasn't sure what he should do, but Michael motioned with his arms for Dave to join him. The notes came quickly and the words were easy enough. Michael spotted a discarded rag in a bush and, continuing to chant, tore it into two strips. He tied one around his upper left arm, and one around Dave's. "That was about freeing the spirit to go on. This one is about listening to our own sadness." Soon Dave entered into the second chant, into the sound and moment, into the great letting go.

When the first of the Cavalry arrived, they found Dave, sitting alone at the picnic table smiling, watching the white Ford Falcon.

Dave Smith would miss the East Fork, but it was time.

V.

Turkey Buzzard swims into view again out of the glare, this time so close I hear his feathers rustle as he banks away and climbs out of reach. He watches me closely. I fight to stay awake and watch him just as closely. It occurs to me that if I am to tell my wife Susie about this, if I am to get off this mountain it will have to be right now.

Right now. Pulling myself up and controlling balance, getting a drink of water, and pulling on my pack and trekking poles, I unsteadily begin the very long walk out. Each step seems to take complete focus. The world shifts back and forth, up and down, a ship in a slow-motion storm. Down through the rocks, the meadows, the clouds of mosquitoes, down through the tall trees and across streams and carpets of blue and yellow, I follow a lifetime of conditioning and put one foot ahead of the next.

Supervisory Verbatim #16

A Last Meeting

When I got to my last scheduled meeting with Dr. Williams, I had to wait for fifteen minutes while he finished his previous session and then wait some more while he brought in a cup of coffee. He looked tired. "There seems to be no end to this business, does there?" I asked.

"It's a real growth industry," he said. "Job security, yes?"

I smiled. "Our clients are just the tip of the iceberg; many more grind away without getting help. Then those that do come into my office or to talk to me in the field, maybe what I do has some effect on them, maybe not. I feel like the guy on the shore throwing starfish back into the ocean the morning after a storm. As many as he could throw, another ten thousand remain. Sometimes it seems pointless."

"But your clients that find themselves in untenable situations—what are their options?" asked Williams. "Fleeing? To where? Failure? Suicide?"

"No! Of course not! They can learn through their hard experiences—sometimes through our help—to change their reactions or how they think about their situations. Or even change the conditions that affect them."

"And in doing so?" he asked.

"Change something in the world."

Dr. Williams gave me his appraising eye. "You don't look finished yet. Is there more?"

"You've asked me why I was drawn to other's pain. . . why I

needed to hold on to the pain in my life."

"Yes, I did. Long ago, when you first started. We've danced around it off and on, but I never felt you were satisfied with your answers. Why can't you drop this line of work? You've been at it for years, done more than most, and we've talked about how it's doing damage to you. Why not drop it all and sell used cars in the 'burbs? Wait tables in San Fernando? Move to Aspen and raise goats?"

"Or at least just be happy," I mused. "Which brings me to my agenda for today. Dr. Williams—Chris—this may be our last session."

"You've made the decision?"

"How did you guess?"

"You've been sending out signs. Questions about the effects your work is having on you. And your family. Then your medical adventure in the mountains. I figured you were working on deciding when to cut your losses."

"I have. I've been thinking of cutting way back on the trauma cases and refocus my practice. I've been doing art more and more. I'd like to work with artists and writers with creative problems or getting beyond writer's block. That sort of thing."

"That makes sense. So what was the point of all the pain for so long?"

"A couple of things, really. Partly to remind me that I have a history. Maybe it's to keep me humble. Maybe a broader purpose."

Williams gave me the eye again. "Like?"

"It got me beyond my concerns. Maybe I was finding a use for what I'd gone through. I want to think that my work has helped the world along a bit. Don't you think your work is like that? You've certainly helped to keep me on track. I appreciate it."

"I'm drawn to working with folks like you. I have my reasons to be drawn to this work. And, like you, I get to play my part. Through you."

Dr. Christopher Williams, Th.D. stood up. "Look, we've talked about it enough. There's a new Brooklyn deli that just opened down the block. Want to get out of here and get some air? I'm hungry."

PART IV

STEPPING DOWN

Retirement both threatened and beckoned. When your identity is tied up in your work, who will you be when you don't? I'd taught for forty years, and of those forty I'd been a practicing therapist for nearly thirty. I'd had my first regular job when I was in seventh grade and worked various types of ranches before I was twenty-one. Work was what I did, and who I was. Stepping down from my work as a trauma therapist did not come easy. On the other hand, it was punching holes in my heart—not the one that pumped blood through my veins, but the one that cried at night. I mourned for the people whose hands I'd held when they shook with fear or convulsed with grief. The ones whom life had slapped down hard. I wept for the times I'd been slapped down, when I'd learned more than I ever wanted to know about how the world floundered around its planetary orbit like the little round ball in a pachinko machine. The stories I'd heard now careened around in my head wreaking havoc on my view of the world and the people around me. I needed to write and to paint and I never had time. I'd always placed a premium on my relationships but now my second wife had just died and my children were strangers. I had health issues. It was time to get out and salvage what I could.

I decided to leave the field of disaster psychology and crisis management. Before I left, however, I needed to pass on some of the things I'd learned along the way—the important things I thought people I'd worked with, or those whose actions affected them, know. This information and these perspectives were needed in order to make reasonable leadership decisions, to give children a chance for full development, and to encourage people to manage the current wave of crises with better understanding. After the conversation with Dr. Williams, I determined that three problems needed to be addressed: the proliferation of assault weapons, the abdication of parental responsibility for protecting their children's childhood, and the need for crisis managers to understand new forces in the world that undermined their efforts. I decided that the best avenue to address these issues lay in writing open letters to three groups, and that I should present these letters in general session conference presentations or publish them in suitable magazines or journals.

Over-controlling? Perhaps; but I couldn't rest easy until I made this last effort.

An Open Letter

To: Members, National Rifle Association
      Members, US House of Representatives
      Members, US Senate

Re: Mass Mayhem

Dear Members,

I write you regarding the escalating mayhem in our streets resulting from the unbridled saturation of weapons in our communities. Many of you may be motivated by lenient interpretations of constitutional rights written under very different circumstance than exist today, pressure by constituents or lobbyists, by pure profit, or by blood lust, but as a crisis consultant who has spent twenty-five years attending to the wounded in body and spirit, I feel I must share some of my experiences walking through the aftermath of your interests and your decisions.

Gun sales are booming and legislation to control gun accessibility appears to be politically stymied. While the majority of arms profit comes from sales of weaponry to our military, there is significant profit in sales to US citizens. Gun sales spiked in the US in 2007, the year the recession hit.

According to the Mother Jones Mass Shootings Database[iii] (which uses a more stringent and conservative

---

iii   Follman, Mark; Aronsen, Gavin; and Pan, Deana. US Mass Shooting, 1982-2019: Data From Mother Jones' Investigation: The full data set from our in-depth investigation into mass shootings. Retrieved from https://www.motherjones.com/politics/2012/12/mass-shootings-mother-jones-full-data/ 8/16/19 set of qualifying criteria than either the FBI or US Congress) there have been 114 public mass shootings since 1982, and the rate of occurrence has roughly tripled in recent years. It should be noted that this means that in each incident at least four human beings were killed, and the killing did not occur in the commission of another crime nor as a result of gang violence. In other words, public shootings involving 3 or less, gang members, or a result of criminal activity were not even counted in the 114 incidents. Nor were the wounded counted in those "non-qualifying" incidents. If you widen the net to include those, you come up with the startling figure of 255 public mass shootings in the first 217 days of 2019[iv]. How you count matters. We can shrug off the numbers by blithely claiming that the shooters are just crazy, but that begs the question of just how crazy we are to arm them.

This descriptive calculus ignores the human and moral dimensions of this discussion. The only ones who would consider this situation acceptable would be those who profit, financially and/or politically on a personal level. To wrap the conversation in either banners or bunting is simply an attempt to hold on to blind power at all cost, a ploy of those who are truly afraid. Your actions serve only to exacerbate the tragedy.

I'd like to include a narrative of some of the highlights (or perhaps low points) of my personal experience as a therapist and on-scene crisis manager as I have attempted to help and heal those who have borne the brunt of your beliefs and policies. To avoid the spectacle of soapbox and sound bite, I am including excerpts of conversations, reflections, and observations of those on the ground I have met on the way. Some of the following narrative is couched

---

iv   Cited by Jason Silverstein, CBS News August 5, 2019 Retrieved from: https://www.cbsnews.com/news/mass-shootings-2019-more-mass-shootings-than-days-so-far-this-year/ 8/17/2019; Source: Gun Violence Archive, Retrieved from: https://www.gunviolencearchive.org/reports/mass-shooting 8/27/19

descriptively, some poetically and some as if it were in the form of a religious service. I am not a particularly religious person, but this seems appropriate for the occasion—A Mass for the Mayhem.

In all sincerity,
Kendall Johnson, Ph.D.

Dr. Johnson's Narrative and Mass for the Mayhem

John (we'll call him that, or her), age 26 (or so), stepped into class for his lecture on Yeats one cold and foggy morning somewhere in Colorado (or one of the other 50 states) on his way to a promising career as something else. Just where he was headed then or later became a moot point when a .30-06 cartridge (or .223, or perhaps .45) hit and killed him instantly.

Oh John! Creative and talented man: father and lover, home from a distant war, retread student with divine aspirations. Charismatic, if somewhat distracted. Listening to a distant music somewhere else—it seems such a waste. One can't help but question the cosmic economics of the God he served.

One heartbeat away from eternity, we live like John at terminal velocity every moment. And yet it all seems so normal, and we make plans, and try to do the right thing as if . . . As if. . .

John who was! Blown into his next life early, thus answering for himself as moot whether it might actually be more noble to suffer the slings and arrows—this fortune indeed outrageous.

*. . . and moot again whether he was to be or not to be
more, or whether despair would eventually dim his bright
spirit. Complete or not, John rests now fully defined—unlike
the rest of us, for whom the jury is still sequestered.*

I'd taken the wrong seat. When I signed up for the threat
assessment class at the Secret Service conference in Las Vegas
as part of my preparation to train one of my crisis teams, I as-
sumed it was going to include school shooters. No such luck.
The emphasis was upon serial killers. School shooters were typ-
ically not serial killers. They were considered "mass murderers."
The enlightenment I needed seemed elusive.

So I went down the hall and took the FBI training class on
Mass Shooting. I found that the FBI considered a mass murder
to be an incident in which four or more victims were killed in
a single incident, whereas Congress required there to be only
three. In the Sandy Hook school shooting in Connecticut in
2012, twenty first-graders and eight adults had been killed.

One speaker pointed out that since Sandy Hook, some "400
people had been shot in over 200 school shootings." Those
figures counted incidents where a single shooter had committed suicide. This hardly qualified as a mass shooting. Another
claimed 300 school shootings since Sandy Hook. The arguments over statistical thresholds seemed less critical to me as
I—entrusted to protect children and teachers—sat listening to
the statisticians, lawyers, and lobbyists for the NRA and other
determined gun advocates.

> *1. Requiem aeternam*
> *Requiem aeternam dona eis, Domine,*
> *et lux perpetua luceat eis.*
> *(4 Esdras ii.34-35)*
> *Grant them eternal rest, O Lord,*
> *and may light eternal shine upon them.*[v]

---

v   English composer John Rutter wrote his Requiem Mass in 1985,

Oklahoma City, 1995. I heard about the bombing first when I was speaking at the World Congress for the crisis management foundation I did consulting for in Baltimore. A colleague and I had just finished our presentation on the development of a novel approach to trauma team training and management we had developed on the West Coast. Emerging from the lecture hall I noticed conference participants—fire, police, military, and emergency medical personnel—gathered around a TV monitor in the lobby. Something serious had just occurred. The incident would eventually involve many of those folks directly.

The Alfred P. Murrah Federal Building in Oklahoma City had been bombed, killing some 168 people and injuring another 680. Hundreds of buildings in a 16-block radius were damaged. It looked and sounded like an air strike or ship-to-shore artillery attack. Later, when I debriefed a fire department search and rescue crisis team, they told me that it was like being in a war zone with piles of concrete and body parts. Up until then we thought terrorists were all from other countries.

2. Out of the deep
> *Out of the deep have I called unto thee,*
> > *Oh Lord.*
> *Lord hear my voice.*
> > > > *Psalm 130*

Oregon, 1998: The evening quiet settled over the college campus, and my class of first responders and school crisis team members gathered closer. We had dispensed with basics and principles and were getting into applications of school crisis management. Cases. It was time to talk about the shooting at Thurston High School two months earlier.

At 8:00 a.m. on the morning in question, the shooter, fifteen

---

mixing basic latin requiem text with Eng-lish versions of Psalms. Retrieved from http://www.windofkeltia.com/requiem/rutter.html August 14, 2019. This was 13 years prior to the first shooting described above.

years old, having already murdered his mother and father at the family home after telling them he loved them, was gearing up in the school parking lot. He slung his automatic rifle, Glock pistols, ammunition clips, and a knife under his trench coat. After passing an acquaintance on his way into the school and suggesting he stay away, the young shooter walked through a passage-way into the central quad area, pulled out his weapons and began firing. Two students were killed and twenty-five wounded before he was wrestled to the ground.

My responders and team members talked about what they had done that day and what they might have done. For them it was about containing the situation and containing the pain. We discussed options, strategies. We considered timing, notifications, staff and student needs, information control.

Then I pressed the team to voice what was really on their minds. "The problem," one said, "was that crowds of kids were standing waiting to watch it go down. They knew in advance it was happening, but no one would tell the police or school authorities."

3. Pie Jesus

Pie Jesu Domine, dona eis requiem sempiternam.
Blessed Lord Jesus, grant them eternal rest.

Colorado, 1999. I stood in front of a crowd of first responders, county mental health and school crisis response team members, and local mental health professions just weeks following the shooting incident at Columbine High School. By any standards the incident was big: 15 died, including 12 students, the shooters and a teacher. 21 were injured. This time I listened to how the two had set bombs in a parking lot to injure incoming rescuers and had credible plans to escape via Stapleton International airport, hijack a commercial plane, and fly it into NYC skyscraper. I learned how the bombs they had set in the cafeteria, had they gone off, would have collapsed the library above into the cafeteria below. This wasn't a school shooting. It was a bombing. Fourteen of their carefully located bombs had detonated, but fortunately the big ones hadn't, due to faulty fuses.

The FBI—via a fact-finding investigative committee including both top incident and behavioral specialists—later announced that more was involved than the prevalent media-inspired myth of goths being persecuted by jocks. Their best guess? The perpetrators were locked in an unholy symbiosis: a violent depressive held under the sway of a determined psychotic.

I recalled a conversation on my way in to Columbine from Stapleton. My driver, a Littleton crisis team member, extolled the virtues of her community. How the neighborhood churches were providing the support to young community members who sought comfort.

4. Agnus Dei

Agnus Dei, qui tollis peccata mundi,
dona eis requiem.
Lamb of God, who takes away the sins of the world,
grant them rest.

California, 2018. I'd hoped I wouldn't get involved. A county mental health clinic in nearby San Bernardino had been attacked by two individuals later identified by the FBI as radicalized Muslims. The clinic was enjoying a Christmas party when the attack occurred. 14 people were killed, 22 wounded by firearms, and many more carried away invisible damage. I got the call a day later to help one of the county employees deal with hidden vulnerability.

In the media storm that followed, one survivor was reported to have commented that while many of the victims sought support from friends and family, some simply disappeared. Another reported that it "breaks her heart" that among her associates who were involved in the incident that day, many who were happy "just aren't happy anymore."

Another newspaper account, this time from one of the victims of the San Bernardino massacre in response to a reporter's question about a subsequent shooting: "Each time there is a shooting it's all we think about. Those who died in the previous incident are forgotten, as are the scores who lost their lives before. Then we go on again."[vi] We have amnesia.

5. *The Lord is My Shepherd*

> *Yea, though I walk*
> *through the valley of the shadow of death,*
> *I will fear no evil,*
> *for thou art with me*

Oregon, 2017. I had gone to high school with Wesley Hurd. He was the football team's quarterback. Now Wes is a theologian and artist in Eugene and he is showing a very interesting collaborative exhibit of his work. Personally affected by the shooting at Umpqua Community College in nearby Roseburg, Oregon on October 1, 2015, Wes dealt with his darkness by launching a set of very large paintings. Nine really big ones that get progressively darker and more nuanced, then turn gradually and suggestively toward hope. His colleague, composer Eliot Grasso saw the emerging work and asked if he could write a musical score to accompany the paintings. Grasso is a musicologist and player of traditional Irish instruments including uilleann pipes. The result of the collaboration, The Odyssey of These Days, premiered on March 3, 2017 at the Hult Center in Eugene.

---

vi   Cited in article by Richard K. De Atley in the San Bernardino Sun November 30, 2018. Retrieved from: https://www.sbsun.com/2018/11/30/with-each-new-mass-shooting-san-bernardino-terror-attack-victims-worry-about-being-forgotten/ 8/17/19

Walking into the dim light of the concert hall, one is confronted by the nine large paintings standing in an open semicircle on the low stage, behind the musical instruments. After words by both Hurd and Grasso, the Breton-inspired lament of abrupt drums, keening pipes, and dissonant fiddles takes us on a journey of anguish, lament, longing, and possibility.

6. *Lux aeterna*

> *Requiem aeternam dona eis Domine,*
> *et lux perpetua luceat eis.*
> *Grant them eternal rest, O Lord,*
> *and may light perpetual shine on them.*

An Open Letter

To: All Parents
       All Teachers

Re: Lamentations

Dear Parents and Teachers,

I have some concerns about our shared future together. These concerns have been growing within me for some time as a result of my having raised, taught, treated, and stabilized your children and mine following crisis events in my capacity as a therapist/consultant. What follows is a transcript of a keynote address I had the privilege of delivering to a statewide conference of psychologists in Lakeland, Florida, a few years ago:

In his novel *The Unbearable Lightness of Being*, Milan Kundera comments on an interaction between two lovers, Franz and Sabina. Sabina had startled Franz by putting a bowler on her head and staring at him. Not knowing what was expected of him, Franz was paralyzed with uncertainty while she waited. The bowler hat had played an extensive role in Sabina's life and in a prior relationship she had with another man. Within the context of the new relationship, the bowler incident was absurd, and experiencing the absurdity, for Sabina, was a measure of the current relationship. As Kundera put it, "They failed to hear the semantic susurrus of the river flowing between them. Without the context of shared experience, it was hard to hear the whisper of meanings that provided the foundation upon which the actions made sense."

And so it is between ourselves and our children's culture—or the anti-culture—that has raised them out from under us, and us out from under ourselves. The susurrus that Kundera talks about is shared experience, a collaborative construction of meaning that forms the foundation underlying present intergenerational discourse. And we are deaf to the more subtle levels of that discourse because it is fraught with tension.

Make no mistake; this is not simply another generation gap. Our children come from a different planet. The world we remember, our past, which we see as so important and for which we feel such sweet nostalgia, has never existed in any significant way for our children.

We are surrounded by a generation of media babies whose sensitivities and sensibilities have been rendered numb. They have become dissociated from the reality to which we are accustomed by an orchestrated assault upon their faculties of perception, conceptualization, valuing, and judgment. Their brains have not been washed, as is sometimes said; rather, they have been shaped beyond recognition. This assault was planned and has been conducted daily throughout their short lives by the finest minds money could buy.

Never mind the obvious blitz of gratuitous violence-qua-style served up to sell itself and other products ranging from perfume to designer clothing to theme parks. One notable full-page advertisement in a hip-hop magazine portrayed a van squealing to a stop in an alley, the passenger leaning out the window and drawing down on several fleeing youths with a shotgun, the label on his pants prominently centered in the photograph. Consider for a moment the more subtle: how the combined talents of toy merchandisers and media sales executives have changed the nature of child's play—their primary developmental work—over the past twenty-five years.

There can be virtue in scarcity. When my son, Trevor, was still confined to a high chair during meals, he would immerse himself in play. Cars and figures would blend with food and eating paraphernalia, often to the detriment of his parents' primary objective: finishing the meal. In desperation, all toys would be removed, and sometimes even dishes and spoons. After one such purging of distractions, I heard the vocalized sounds of an intense car race coming from the kitchen. The "vroom-vrooms" of a dead heat past the vegetables caused me to go after the forbidden toy car that must have escaped the shake-down. But when I got there, the only thing on the tray was a single pea, being pushed by the end of a spoon. Trevor was pushing it about with enough accompanying noise to make Mario Andretti feel at home. For the true purposes of play, less is usually more.

Play has been changed by the marketplace in some very unhealthy ways. The objects and artifacts of play were simple. Traditionally, play was spontaneous and make-do; it was creative, with its critical lack of definition opening the way for infinite interpretations, rules, and possibilities. Like my son's pea, the energy and joy came from within. Today play comes pre-packaged with a glitz and flash that covers a very limited set of player's options of response. The objects and artifacts of play are provided, and what can be done with them is largely predetermined. Further, automated games that incorporate others do so in a "virtual" way: the "person" incorporated to play with you is no more than a bundle of set response options allowed by the game. You, in turn, as incorporated into another's game, are simply a bundle of response options that you are allowed by the game. In other words, the "you" and the "other" are not real in the game context. You are both virtual, artificial persons.

Fantasy always permeates play. But in traditional play, the fantasy had to be added to the mix, like water to dehydrated powder. Contemporary entertainment and play incorporate, co-opt, and limit the fantasy. Designers define the fantasy and determine the response options. The initial idea may be attractive—more so than home-grown toys—

but take the game to its limits, and it is just that: limited. Gone is personal interpretation and authorship.

Another crucial difference between traditional play and contemporary entertainment is the context within which the play is enacted. Because traditional play was frequently interactive, it necessarily involved considerable social skill development. Communication and conflict resolution were critical to play's success. Not so with most current entertainment and play. Videos, video-games, electronic games, and most of today's toys are to be played alone, or at least played with virtual partners even when on-line. If those played with are allowed only options limited by the parameters allowed by the program—however varied—they are not allowed fully human response. To the extent they are interactive, the interaction is prefabricated and mostly competitive. But the developmental problem here is deeper.

The interaction in most traditional play was value-infused, as it reflected the world in which it took its origins. Most contemporary play treats valuational issues as if they were neutral. Killing is simulated, hence OK. While John Wayne was, at times, brutal, he was brutal in defense of community standards. If two children couldn't resolve an issue arising in a game, they lost the chance to play. Or even worse, they took days, or even months to work out the interpersonal breach between them. Much of the violence in contemporary media is not just gratuitous, but stylistic. Violence for violence sake becomes an art form. But even more importantly, the interaction in traditional play always bore consequences. The vast majority of today's media and games portray violence as being at best instrumental, at worse without any serious consequence. Even hard-hearted trainers of snipers point out that under the conditions of contemporary media play, impulses of a moral nature are deconditioned. The vast, overriding message to today's children is that it doesn't really matter what you do.

Psychologist John Dewey, like much of value today, is

dead but not forgotten. His perspective is very helpful when we consider the broad effects of play and the manipulation of play. He considered perception, indeed reality itself, to be a constructive act between the perceiver and that which they perceived. The world (as opposed to the planet) is constructed anew every day as we make meaning of our experience. Thus our world is only as rich, exciting, worthwhile, and laden with potential we make it. In this sense, our primary responsibility as parents, and as cultural decision-makers, is to allow our children to strengthen their skills as constructors of fulfilling lives. Play is the process by which children learn to construct real worlds.

What violence do we inflict, then, when we allow others to constrict our children's learning and development? What violence do we do our children by raising them into a meaningless world, bound by limits imposed by a merchandised consciousness? Our children face a world right now that makes *1984*, George Orwell's novel about totalitarian thought control, not only plausible but half materialized. The barbarians have entered the gates, and we let them in. Perhaps we have become them.

And if our children's contemporary play—their primary form of learning—inherently limits their powers of volition and creativity, look what it does to their moral and social development. Let me tell you about the mother of one of my son's friends when my son was 16.

When I stopped to pick my son up, his mother came to intercept me. "They'll just be a few minutes," she explained. "I want them to run an extra copy of their science project report."

Because I didn't want to take my shoes off, a custom at their house to prevent dirt from coming in, I chose to wait at the door. My waiting was obviously a problem for her. She wanted to buy time for them to do some more work by engaging me in conversation.

"I'm just afraid they won't get it done before Thursday."

"Well, if they don't, it's pretty much on their shoulders," I ventured.

"Oh, no!" she replied. "It's on mine. I work closely with him on all his homework. I always have. It would be my failure!"

I thought for a minute. Earlier, my son had pointed out with some amazement how the mother had carefully shown them how to cut segments of articles out of web-sites and paste them into their science report.

"I wonder how his first year at college is going to be. He's probably in for a big surprise."

"No, he's not," she exclaimed. "He's going to go to the colleges here. He'll live at home. You know," she added, "I may not be too smart, but I've got one thing going for me. Ambition." And she did. Fancy house, painfully clean; designer clothes. Face-lift. Strained smile.

I had always thought of my son's friend as slightly larval, almost shapeless; no feeling registered on his face. No evidence of character or even personality. This all made a certain discomforting sense. Later, I asked my son about it.

"He's really into guns," he pointed out. "Belongs to the NRA. The word around campus is that his web site is full of guns, violence, and hate. Makes lots of threats."

Will he act on his threats? Who knows.

Is it a possibility? You bet.

His world admitted no others. He would be spoon-fed through college and be raised within the family business. He would inherit the very clean house.

Is there a connection between his potential for violence and his mother's consuming "ambition?" I'm not sure, but I have uncomfortable feelings that there might be.

My son's friend stands as a caricature of a generation. Self-centered, interested only in immediate gratification, unable to generate true creativity or personal imagination, immune to concerns about the larger human family. From the point of view that sees the importance of this young man's developing ability to construct a real and satisfying world, he can certainly be considered a victim of cultural violence. He and many, many like him.

There are not enough gun detectors, miles of razor wire, or armed security guards to protect our campuses from threats from within. Nor can we be expected to bring the violence to an end by adding on a class in conflict resolution or character development. It goes far deeper than walkie-talkies and psychological band-aids.

The Eric Klebolds and Andy Williamses of the world cannot be left alone to ravage our schools. But before we write them off with self-satisfied, presidential pronouncements like "disgraceful act of cowardice" and "our thoughts are with you," let's pause for a moment and consider from whence the shooters came. It takes more than a dysfunctional family to raise a shooter. As a politician rightly proclaimed: "It takes a whole village."

Bodies mount up. What used to be a school event now knows no boundaries of age or place. From Post Office to sidewalks, from dance halls to techno-glitter bars, a new terror is becoming more commonplace. Extreme violence in public places is simply the outer edge breakdown of the thin veneer holding us all together. It isn't young people breaking down; it is all of us.

An Open Letter

To: Class I & Class II Incident Commanders

Re: Farewell

I hope this finds you all safe and well. It's been a real pleasure and honor to be able to serve you over the past twenty-five or so years on fire lines and Incident Command posts around the country. This is to let you know that I am hereby retiring from my work with you. We've always joked about wanting to meet under better circumstances, and now, should we meet, the circumstances will be far better than they have been in the past.

Those of you who know me know that I can't help but give out more advice. Please bear with me as this may be my last shot with you folks. Some of you may also remember me dispensing with similar information at an Incident Commander conference a few years ago. Indulge me if you will; I care deeply for each of you and what you do. I couldn't sleep at night if I didn't say these words again.

My purpose is to lay out some things I have noticed during my years of wandering through I.C.s as an invited consultant. The first has to do with stress. I've heard command stress characterized as consequential decision making, based upon inadequate information, with limited and inadequate resources, when you're too tired to think clearly, and everyone else is too.

In general, that's what I mean by difficult circumstances. I want to look at these, starting with the changing nature and context of large incidents.

The Changing Nature of Large Incidents

Technological developments aside, how much have large incidents changed over the time I've been involved in them? A great deal and not all of it has to do with organization, tactics, and equipment.

Disaster management has always dealt with the very worst of situations. Lately, however, the disasters have been as much about the changing times as they have been about natural events. I believe you will agree with me that the incidents you manage today have escalated significantly in terms of their complexity and complications. Some specific factors include:

- Budgetary constraints in the face of increased scope and expense
- The ever-present threat of litigation
- A backdrop of political/social instability
- Voracious media attention giving new meaning to the phrases "damage control" and "creating its own weather."
- A less obvious cultural shift changing the very meaning of the events themselves

Some recent examples:

Disaster: Sichuan Province Earthquake, 2008

> 70k fatalities in region (*how many 9/11s is that?*)
> 7000 school rooms collapsed
> Physical infrastructural collapse

A disaster of unprecedented proportions. Each township, each city block a Class-I incident. Yet at that ground-level, there was more to the event, and managing public reaction to the event on scene, than met the eye. Pictures show side-by-side buildings where one collapsed and the other did not. The public buildings constructed during periods of political and economic transition collapsed more often. The possibility of graft affected the neighborhood's reaction to the collapse, and the rescue crews had to deal with those neighbors.

The point of discussing this with you is to give you an illustration of the social and political dimensions as they affect incident management.

Another incident: consider the <u>Beslan School siege in North Ossetia</u> in 2004

The event itself was horrifying enough:

- Terrorists took an entire school hostage—1,100 people (777 were children)
- Gun battle—reports differ as to exactly who or what started it.
- A mess: 334 dead (186 children)
- More mess: controversy over the use of force.
- Again, a political firestorm of international proportion.
- Russian Security Forces were accused of excessive force.

The New Context of Large Incidents

My second point for you is the changing context of incident management. This point requires a bit of sociological and theoretical clarification, but there is no crystal ball rubbing necessary. What we face is a present danger, but it is in no way clear. This new century is indeed a new era: a socio/political soup. There's so much mixed up that we can't tell what's in it and we can't see the bottom. Speaking technically and clinically, SNAFU is turning to FUBAR faster than we can keep it sorted.

Here are some elements in this soup that I see in play now:

- Budget cutbacks vs more incidents
- More caused by humans
- Greater expectation on governmental agencies
- Political drama as a "new normal"
- The incendiary effects of sensationalist media coverage

So what happened? How'd we get this far off the trail? That calls for some theory. Bear with me for a moment, because I do feel that it is relevant for each of you to think about. It has to do with the context within which you work—it affects your stress levels, and it sets the stage for your on-scene interpersonal communication.

Part of our response to a situation is determined by what it means to us. While we'd like to surround ourselves with "Professional Detachment," and usually we try to, we cannot remain unmoved by the human drama that surrounds us. In particular, when we are deeply fatigued, our resistance to the intensity of situations weakens. That's when the meaning of the event takes on a personal valence. And this process is sometimes very tricky.

Today we work within a context of high drama. Incidents can come to carry personal meaning, but they also have meaning for society. And to complicate things, there are both surface meanings and meanings below the surface.

SURFACE MEANING:

Crises, violence, and disasters *de-stabilize* the wider community, but under the choppy surfaces of that water, run deeper and stronger currents.

SUB-SURFACE MEANING:

The incidents we respond to are complex and difficult. But they are coming to carry a symbolic meaning as well. They *represent* more subtle social, political, cultural and historical chaos afoot in the world.

There are a lot of things happening in our world—rapidly changing economies, terrorism, the destruction of things we believed in, cyclonic changes in culture and values—that we have no control over.

So the spectacle of the armies of light—that would be you folks—going off to fight the evil forces of chaos—Fire, Wind, Water—takes on a literary, indeed a cinematic, magnitude.

In other words, disaster becomes theater. What used to be a shared threat within the public sphere now becomes a drama and the whole world watches what you do (as do those who hold your budget)! No wonder you feel a little pressure now and then. And like all good fiction, there are sub-plots within sub-plots.

To understand why you feel the heat, we might take a little broader visual reconnaissance. Let's ask ourselves who has what to gain from dramatizing emergencies that bring grief to others. While you folks have your shoulders to the mill-stone—making plans, arranging facilities, ordering up equipment, and deploying teams—other folks with different priorities are also taking position. Some of these vested interests are economic, some political, and some ideological.

And sometimes things go on that nobody plans, or even understands how they play into a process. Maybe most people don't spend as much time in reflection as you folks spend in thinking about strategies and priorities, but when we try to make sense of how things have gotten so confusing, we often don't see our own role in aiding and abetting the confusion. So it is with spectacle.

Certain theorists have pointed out how our quest for a little diversion, a little entertainment and interest to relieve the anxieties of contemporary life, have ended up becoming an obsession. In 1967, Guy Debord talked about what now seems a pretty tame social phenomena. He claimed that "spectacles" (scandals, conflicts, consumer fads) divert public attention away from politically uncomfortable realities.

His idea was called "Spectacle Theory." Five years ago another spectacle theorist extended this approach to consider how technical developments and increased marketing have taken Debord's ideas to places even he never considered. This new theorist pointed out what all of us know—that the biggest spectacle is mass media. Mass media functions to create spectacles through entertainment, television, internet, blogs, tweets, etc., at an escalating rate.

Here's the bottom line: if you are on an incident in Southern California, for instance, and something goes wrong, there's a pretty good chance that much of the nation may hear about it before you do. I know many of you have been involved in incident-related fatalities where the family received notification by a reporter. Folks like Judy Dowling in Billings are working at using social media to counter some of the social effects of the technological virus plaguing incident management. Her work is bearing fruit and many emergency agencies across the country are taking advantage of social media to deliver accurate information regarding developing incidents, traffic, evacuation routes, and safe havens.

The media is only one aspect of the analysis of the spectacle nature of large incidents, but it's big enough for our discussion. I don't have to quote researchers on it: you know how the media ramps up your stress level, whether or not you are the Public Information Officer. How does that feel? How would you describe it in terms of a commander's lived experience?

While you are dealing boots on the ground with the situation, it transforms into something else, becoming, in Douglas Kellner's words: "the transformation of the public sphere into a mere show, a spectacle for audiences, not for citizens."

Bottom line: the context of your work affects the stress level generated by that work. What used to be a fairly simple process of "putting wet on red" or containing chaos becomes far more stressful when contaminated by media and political spectacle used by outside forces to promote their agenda.

Stress and Command Communication

The last point I want to make has to do with the effects of stress on command communication. How do the tires of all this social theory meet the road of incident management? How does the FUBAR of these changed circumstances set the stage for communication SNAFU? Incident Management, particularly within today's context, is by its very nature stressful. That isn't going away. Nor will all the deep breathing exercises, vitamins, and pleasant thoughts, give you an extra 2 hours sleep or chase the TV commentators away. But good communication can help.

Paul Gleason, legendary fire god and safety guru of the

wildland fire agencies, wrote, "Distraction is a very real problem for firefighters. Fatigue and carbon monoxide do not help with the decision making process either." He wasn't just talking about fires. I first met Paul in late spring 1964 in the Dalton Hot Shots where he was lead hook. That fall we stood at fire camp on the Coyote Fire in Santa Barbara, watching helicopters landing near a line of ambulances, unloading a contract hand crew who had been burned over. From the first, Paul was always concerned about fire safety, and about communication and heads-up decision making. He never forgot that lesson, reinforced on the Loop fire and later in Colorado, as he moved his way up to become Deputy Fire Management Officer for the NPS's Rocky Mountain Region. He developed fire safety concepts still in use. Paul finally rose to a teaching position at Colorado State University.

Obviously his work was about more than fire. As Paul pointed out, "[Incident] personnel should be continually monitoring each other and remain open to communication and others evaluation of the situation at hand." This is, in short, mindfulness.

Paul spoke words of wisdom, and his ideas were all learned the hard way. Paul is no longer with us, and he is missed. Sadly, while you may not miss me—especially given the circumstances when I'd usually show up—it's time I hung up my hard hat as well. I am retiring this year. You've been a special part of my life and I will miss you. Thanks for your patience in hearing me out, and allowing me to speak with you. I wish you all of the best—the best weather, the best luck, all the resources you need, and a press blackout—and all of the deep satisfaction that can come from your very important work together.

Thank you and please be safe out there.
Kendall Johnson

EPILOGUE

A Ritual of Healing

1.

Called now to ritual attunement
our souls come together to work
in redwood forest evening.
Seven crows circling high
celebrate our passage across
river on suspended bridge.

*   *   *

2.

Incantations whispered down
generations as black arm band
affix and externalize our fears.
We walk swaying and balancing
between like fears, declaring
our own as truly our own.

*   *   *

3.

At midway we push through
red shrouds of sin re-birthing
into billowing white shrouds.
Incantations again at bridges end
mark and open beginnings.
We circle into chant.

*   *   *

4.

Embraced and pulled forward
winding through ancient redwoods
we enter sacred ceremonial ground
circled by poles, half black
enshrouded, half white
with stark crimson accent.

*   *   *

5.

"Here there are no wrong notes
no wrong words" you intoned.
We invoked spirits and powers
sudden winds answered.
We invoked death and we
were circled by black ravens.

*   *   *

6.

Into the circle of wise elders
we confessed shameful fears
voices blending to one sound
and through the common song
of painful admission
we each were heard.

*   *   *

7.

Ancient trees grew upward
on each side of the water
above the ribbon of celestial fire
reflected in the river below;
the heavens listened,
we each were heard.

*   *   *

8.

And with those waters and birds
and gathering darkness and
drums and fire and chants
and one another, we began healing.
The long walk starts
with a step toward each other.

*   *   *

9.

Benedictions finally closing
We found ourselves again ready
attuned to one another and world
and ourselves. We one hundred
waking into this world again.

*   *   *

10.

Together on the banks
of that indigo river;
seeing one other
for the first time again,
the river rushes around us
and freely in between.

*   *   *

About the Author

Kendall Johnson, former firefighter with military experience, served as traumatic stress consultant—often in the field—specializing in Incident Command System Class I & II commands. Initially working with individual and small team line per-sonnel, His responsibilities evolved to provide consultation to field commanders and their operational teams, and, when necessary, provide intervention in order to maintain team effectiveness in the midst of incidents that had turned traumatic. He has lectured in fire houses, hospitals, emergency service institutes, conferences, government training facilities, universities, here and abroad.

He trained others in the principles he developed. Dr. Johnson was Adjunct Faculty member at the California State Training Institute (Governor's Office of Emergency Services), served on the Faculty of the International Critical Incident Stress Foundation, and was Associate Professor in the Master's Degree program in Emergency Services Management at California State University, Long Beach.

He has authored a number of professional papers, seven books in the treatment of traumatic stress, school crisis management, and recovery. Recently Dr. Johnson retired from teaching to pursue painting, photography, and writing. In that capacity he has written five literary books of artwork and poetry, and one in art history.

www.ingramcontent.com/pod-product-compliance
Lightning Source LLC
Chambersburg PA
CBHW031347020726
47499CB00005B/1428